# EUROPEAN INTEGRATION

## THEORIES AND APPROACHES

EDITED BY
HANS J. MICHELMANN
PANAYOTIS SOLDATOS



UNIVERSITY PRESS OF AMERICA

Lanham • New York • London

**University Press of America,® Inc.**
4720 Boston Way
Lanham, Maryland 20706

3 Henrietta Street
London WC2E 8LU England


Printed in the United States of America
British Cataloging in Publication Information Available

**Library of Congress Cataloging-in-Publication Data**

European integration : theories and approaches / edited by
Hans J. Michelmann and Panayotis Soldatos.
p. cm.
Includes bibliographical references.
1. Europe—Economic integration. 2. Europe 1992. 3. European
Economic Community. I. Michelmann, Hans J. II. Soldatos,
Panayotis.
HC241.E816 1994 337.1'4—dc20 94-984 CIP

ISBN 0-8191-9455-7 (pbk. : alk. paper)

The paper used in this publication meets the minimum requirements of American National Standard for Information Sciences—Permanence of Paper for Printed Library Materials, ANSI Z39.48-1984.

# EUROPEAN INTEGRATION: THEORIES AND APPROACHES

Sous la direction de / Edited by

Hans J. MICHELMANN and Panayotis SOLDATOS

Canadian Council for European Affairs/
Conseil Canadien des Affaires Européennes

# PREFACE

The idea for this volume had its genesis some years ago. At the time of the events leading to Europe 1992 and the Maastricht Treaty, a number of scholars were wondering if the old theories of European integration, fallen largely into disrepute, could use a dusting off and another look, if not a reinterpretation. At any rate, the idea of a volume on theories and approaches to European integration appeared to the two editors as timely, and hence we set our minds to deciding on authors.

We chose to organize the volume around the academic disciplines which have dealt with the topic and to allow specialists in these disciplines, or scholars thoroughly familiar with them, to present the theories and approaches that characterize their literature on European integration. Two of the chapters, those by Pierre-Henri Laurent and Alex J. Easson on historical perspectives and legal approaches, respectively, had previously appeared in the *Journal of European Integration*, a journal co-edited by the editors of the present volume.[1] They were revised for this volume. A third chapter, that by Alfred Tovias on economic theories of European integration, was published in a recent issue of the journal and hence did not require updating.[2]

Our first debt of gratitude, then, is to the authors themselves and their patience with us in our attempts to publish a complete volume on theories and approaches to European integration. We are grateful to the two authors of the chapters published some years ago in the *Journal of European Integration* for their diligence in updating their work, and to those who joined us subsequently for the timely manner in which they produced their manuscripts. We wish to thank the Canadian Council for European Affairs and its donor organizations, particularly the Ottawa Delegation of the Commission of the European Community, for helping to finance the editorial costs of this volume and for subsidizing its publication. Mary Frances Schmidt expertly prepared the camera-ready manuscript. Special thanks are due to the publishers and staff of the University Press of America for not losing patience with the editors after numerous delays in completing this volume.

Hans J. Michelman
Panayotis Soldatos

---

[1]The chapters appeared as articles in Volume XII, nos. 2-3 of the journal.

[2]It was published in Volume XV, no. 1.

# THE HARD CORE OF EUROPEAN INTEGRATION THEORIES AND APPROACHES: A MULTIVARIATE TRACK OF VARIABLE GEOMETRY

Hans J. Michelmann
*University of Saskatchewan*

Panayotis Soldatos
*University of Montreal*

A close examination of the various approaches to theorizing about European integration since World War II reveals a rich and varied record of intellectual activity. Such an examination can be organized around two perspectives: one focusing on the evolution of the phenomena associated with the European Community itself and of the related theoretical endeavors, and one focusing on a critical evaluation of theorizing on European integration and on the evolution of the academic disciplines involved in the process of theorizing.

## I. THEORIZING ABOUT AN EVOLUTIONARY PHENOMENON OF VARIABLE GEOMETRY

As in all attempts at rigorous theorizing, that focusing on European integration is closely tied to the complex evolution of the phenomenon as well as the variable geometry of its architecture. Different developments at the Community level have led to a varied and rich theoretical literature:

- The attempts to explain the unique phenomenon that constitutes the process of European integration gave birth to neofunctionalism, an approach whose roster of explanantory variables was able to transcend the somewhat limited list of historial and political determinants identified by Karl W. Deutsch and his collaborators.[1]

---

[1] Among the contributions attempting to explain the phenomenon of international integration are the following: J. BARREA, *L'intégration politique externe: notion globale et analyse sociologique*, Louvain, Paris, 1969; K.W. DEUTSCH et al., *Political Community and the North Atlantic Area: International Organization in the Light of Historical Experience*, Princeton, 1957; E.B. HAAS and P. SCHMITTER, Economics and Differential Patterns of Political Integration, *International Organization*, no. 4 (1964), pp. 705–737; J.S. NYE, *Peace in Parts*, Boston, 1970; and P. SOLDATOS, *Vers une sociologie de l'intégration européenne*, Louvain, 1973.

- For its part, the institutional architecture of the European Community has been the object of numerous types of theorizing. Among these are neofunctionalism with its emphasis on a system of mixed elites and on the organization of a common decision making center, as well as the juridico-institutional approach focusing on the supranationality of the institutional and decision making systems. Federalism, another line of theorizing, emphasizes increases in political integration, on the one hand, and explores, on the other, the power sharing relations between the center and member states.[2]
- The evolutionary dynamics of the European integration process, its rationality and its rhythm, attracted the attention of both economists and the theorists of neofunctionalist spillover. The former have allowed us to identify the imperatives which underlie the various integrative stages (free trade zone, customs union, common market and economic union); the latter have suggested a multidisciplinary model of linkages, taking into account the political and institutional, socio-cultural, economic and attitudinal forces that propel the process of integration towards its more developed stages.[3]

---

[2]See, in particular: J. MÉGRET *et al.*, *Le Droit de la Communauté économique européenne*, Brussels, 1979 *et suiv.*; V. CONSTANTINESCO, *Compétences et pouvoirs dans les Communautés européennes*, Paris, 1974; P. HAY, *Federalism and Supranational Organizations*, Chicago, 1966; T.C. HARTLEY, *The Foundation of European Community Law*, 1981; R. LECOURT, *L'Europe des juges*, Brussels, 1976; H. LESGUILLONS, *L'application d'un traité-fondation: le traité instituant la CEE*, Paris, 1968; J.-V. LOUIS, *L'ordre juridique communautaire*, Brussels, 1985; S. NERI, *La nature juridique des Communautés européennes*, 1965; J. RAUX, *Les relations extérieures de la CEE*, 1966; M. TORELLI, *L'individu et le droit de la CEE*, Montreal, 1970; E. WALL, *Europe: Unification and Law*, 1960. See also the bibliographic references in the chapter by A. EASSON in this volume.

[3]On the theorizing on the continuum of different phases of integration see, in particular, B. BALASSA, *The Theory of Economic Integration*, Homewood, Ill., 1961. For the neofuntionalist contribution to the theory of spillover see, most notably: E.B. HAAS, *The Uniting of Europe: Political, Social and Economic Forces, 1950–1957*, Stanford, 1958; E.B. HAAS, *Beyond the Nation State*, Stanford, 1964; E.B. HAAS and P. SCHMITTER, Economic and Differential Patterns of Political Integration, *loc. cit.*; E.B. HAAS, Technocracy, Pluralism and the New Europe, in S. GRAUBARD (ed.), *A New Europe?*, Cambridge, 1964, pp. 82–88; E.B. HAAS, The Uniting of Europe and the Uniting of Latin America, *Journal of Common Market Studies*, 1967, no. 4, pp. 315–343; E.B. HAAS, *The Obsolescence of Regional Integration Theory*, Berkeley, 1975; R.D. HANSEN, Regional Integration, *World Politics*, 1962, no. 2, pp. 242–274; R.D. HANSEN, European Integration, *International Organization*, 1973, no. 3, pp. 225–291; J.S. NYE, *Peace in Parts, op. cit.;* P. SCHMITTER, Three Neofunctionalist Hypotheses about International Integration, *International Organization*, 1969 and Further Notes on Operationalizing

- The creation by the European Community of a politial system nourished by the attitudes and behavior of individual actors, elites, groups and political as well as economic forces, led to a type of sociological theorizing focusing on the various mechanisms supporting the Comunity system and a literature that developed effective measuring instruments.[4]
- The progressive development of Community policies inspired the development of theorizing with regard to policy making and the

---

some Variables Related to Regional Integration, *International Organization,* 1964, no. 4, pp. 705–37; and C. PENTLAND, *International Theory and European Integration,* London, 1973.

[4]With respect to attitudes and behaviors see, in particular, K.W. DEUTSCH, *Nationalism and Social Communications: An Inquiry into the Foundations of Nationality*, New York, 1953; *Idem., Political Community at the International Level: Problems of Definition and Measurement*, New York, 1954; *Idem., The Nerves of Government: Models of Political Communications and Control,* New York, 1963; *Idem.,* Communications Theory and Political Integration, in P. JABOCS and J. TOSCANO (eds.), *The Integration of Political Communities,* New York, 1964; *Idem.,* The Impact of Communications upon International Relations Theory, in A. SAID (ed.), *Theory of International Relations: The Crisis of Relevance*, 1968; *Idem., Alliance: Europe Faces Coming Policy Decisions,* New York, 1967; and K.W. DEUTSCH *et al., France, Germany and the Western Alliance: A Study of Elite Attitudes on European Integration and World Politics,* New York, 1967. See also, R. INGLEHART, Public Opinion and Regional Integration, *International Organization,* 1970, no. 4, pp. 764–795; *Idem.,* The New Europeans: Inward or Outward Looking? *International Organization* 1970, no. 1, pp. 129–139; *Idem.,* Cognitive Mobilization and European Identity, *Comparative Politics,* 1970, no. 1, pp. 45–70; *Idem.,* La fin de l'intégration européenne? in D. SIDJANSKI, (ed.), *Méthodes quantitatives et intégration européenne,* Geneva, 1970; J.-R. RABIER, Les attitudes des Européens à l'égard de l'unification de l'Europe, *European Studies Newsletter,* 1973, no. 3, pp. 10–18; *Idem.,* L'opinion des Européens sur les aspects régionaux et agricoles du Marché commun: l'unification politique de l'Europe et l'information du public, Brussels, 1971; *Idem.,* Les Européens et l'unification de l'Europe, 1972; *Idem.,* L'Europe est bien vue par les Européens, 1974; *Idem.,* L'étude de l'opinion publique européenne, *Revue d'intégration européenne/Journal of European Integration,* 1978, no. 3; *Idem.,* The Evolution of Public Attitudes toward European Integration, *ibid.,* 1987, nos. 2-3, pp. 277–288; K. REIF and R. INGLEHART (eds.), *Eurobarometer: The Dynamics of European Public Opinion-Essays in Honour of Jacques-René Rabier*, London, 1991; see on political parties: F. BORRELLA, *Les partis politiques dans l'Europe des Neuf,* Paris, 1979; P.H. CLAES and N. LOEB-MAYER, Trans-European Party Groupings, *Government and Opposition,* 1979, no. 4, pp. 455–478; D. SEILER, *Partis and familles politiques,* Paris, 1980.

The literature on pressure groups includes J. MEYNAUD and D. SIDJANSKI, *Les groupes de pression dans la Communauté européenne,* Brussels, 1971; D. SIDJANSKI and U. AYBERK, Bilan des groupes et du processus de décision dans la Communauté des Six, *Res Publica,* 1974, no. 1, pp. 33–36 and *Idem.,* Le nouveau visage des groupes d'intéret communautaires, *Revue d'intégration européenne/Journal of European Integration,* 1987, nos. 2–3, pp. 172–201.

exploration of schemes that could explain the relationship between policy making at the European and at the national levels.[5]

- The preoccupation with European integration as a dependent variable instigated systematic "*polity*-oriented" theorizing.[6]
- The initiation of a process that created a single market and moved toward an economic and monetary union introduced into the literature micro-economic and macro-economic approaches to theorizing.[7]
- The development of a globalized economy and the European Community's reaction to the phenomena associated with this trend led to the need for new attempts to explain the EC's new global role using concepts such as "the world systems approach," externalization, the interdependence of regional blocs, but also to a renewed emphasis on the more traditional analysis of the EC's role in international trade.[8]

---

[5]See in particular the contributions by H. WALLACE *et al.* (eds.), *Policy-Making in the European Community*, London, 1983 as well as the two publications by ECSA-US: L. HURWITZ and C. LEQUESNE (eds.), *The State of the European Community,* Boulder, Col., 1991; A.W. CAFRUNY and G.G. ROSENTHAL, *The State of the European Community* (Part 4), Boulder Col., 1993 (forthcoming).

[6]See particularly the works by E.B. HAAS, L.N. LINDBERG and J.S. NYE, previously cited.

[7]B. BALASSA, *op. cit.*; P. CECHINI *et al., 1992, le défi: nouvelles données économiques de l'Europe sans frontières*, Paris, 1988; G.S. DENTON (ed.), *Economic Integration in Europe,* London, 1969; H. GIERSCH, *Integration durch Währungsunion,* Tübingen, 1971; R. LIPSEY, *The Theory of Customs Unions: A General Equilibrium Analysis,* London, 1970; A. MARCHAL, *L'Europe solidaire,* Paris, 1964; W. MOLLE, *The Economics of European Integration,* Portsmouth, 1990; J. NEME and C. NEME, *Économie européenne*, Paris, 1970; J. PELKMANS *et al., Europe's Domestic Market,* 1986; F. PERROUX, *L'Europe sans rivages,* Paris, 1954; L. REBOUD, *L'achèvement du Marché commun intérieur,* Paris, 1987; D. SWANN, *The Economics of the Common Market*, Hammondsworth (various editions); J. TINBERGEN, *International Economic Integration,* London and New York, 1965; L. TSOUKALIS, *The Politics and Economics of European Monetary Integration,* London, 1977; *Idem, Europe, America and the World,* Brugge, 1986; J. VINER, *The Customs Union Issue,* New York, 1950.

[8]See, in particular, J.A CAPORASO, The European Community in the World System, *Revue d'intégration européenne/Journal of European Integration*, 1974, no. 3, pp. 415–440; J. GALTUNG, *Europe: A Superpower in the Making*, London, 1973; F. LAURSEN (ed.), *Europe 1992, World Partner? The International Market and the World Political Economy,* Maastricht, 1991; C. PENTLAND, Linkage Politics: Canada's Contract and the Development of the European Community's External Relations, *International Journal*, 1977, no. 2; *Idem., The External Relations of the European Community: Three Perspectives and their Implications for Canada,* paper presented at the Kingston Conference on Canada and the European Community;

- The arduous but unrelenting thrust of the EC toward the "high politics" of a common foreign and security policy has highlighted the need to transcend previous approaches in order to find an effective means of theorizing about this para-Community system of political cooperation, which is, perhaps, best accounted for in regime theory.[9]
- The segmentation of member states resulting from European integration and international interdependence, on the one hand, and by the aspirations for a structural-functional decentralization of the nation state as expressed by subnational actors (federated units, regions, cities), on the other, have induced theoreticians of European integration to analyze the "EC-member state-subnational" actors triangle, highlighting a new societal stucturing "beyond and within the nation state"[10]
- Institutional and political spillover in the EC since the Single European Act and the Maastricht Treaty have led to a re-examination of the new EC system.[11]

It is through this multiplication of approaches that the present collectively written volume undertakes to provide to the reader a selective and multidisciplinary presentation of the theorizing about European integration by virtue of contributions that, without claiming to be exhaustive of the subject, concentrate on the "hard core" of the various academic disciplines and their related theoretical approaches.

---

*Idem.*, L'évolution de la politique étrangère de la Communauté européenne: le contexte transatlantique, *Études internationales,* 1978, no. 1, pp. 106–112; J. RAVENHILL, *Collective Clientelism: The Lomé Convention and North-South Relations,* New York, 1985; L. THUROW, *Head to Head: The Coming Economic Battle among Japan, Europe and America*, 1992.

[9]See most notably the theoretical contributions in M. HOLLAND (ed.), *The Future of European Political Cooperation,* London, 1991.

[10]See especially the contributions of the special issue of the *Revue d'intégration européenne/Journal of European Integration*, 1992, nos. 2–3; M. BONNEVILLE *et al., Villes européennes et internationalisation*, Lyon, 1992; and C. MILLON-DELSOL, *L'État subsidiaire,* Paris, 1992.

[11]See, in particular, R.O. KEOHANE and S. HOFFMANN (eds.), *The New European Community*, Boulder, Col., 1991; J. LODGE, *The Democratic Deficit and the European Community*, London, 1991; L. TSOUKALIS, *The New European Economy: The Politics and Economics of Integration*, Paris, 1992; and D. SIDJANSKI, *L'avenir fédéraliste de l'Europe: la Communauté européenne des origines au traité de Maastricht*, Paris, 1993.

## II. TOWARDS A CRITICAL EVALUATION OF THEORIZING ON EUROPEAN INTEGRATION

After forty years of European integration and attendant theorizing, a loss of vigor in theoretical reflection can be detected.[12] Neofunctionalism has not succeeded in leading us to post-neofunctionalism, while at the same time, certain other approaches, more relevant in the last quarter of this century (for example, the "world system," "international complex interdependence," "subnational actors" and "international regimes" approaches) have not succeeded sufficiently in focusing on European integration to suggest new theoretical points of departure.

Given this crisis of ideas, we limit ourselves here to underlining certain central weaknesses of the neofunctionalist "hard core" theorizing on European integration. First, most of the important works on European integration lack a broad comparative basis: they dedicate themselves to theorizing about integration in one of the regions of the international system, viz., Western Europe; and the absence of cases comparable to supranational integration in the EC has led neofunctionalism to establish its list of conditions through a comparative analysis of organizations of cooperation-integration that vary strongly in terms of types of integration, institutions, final objectives, geographical contexts, socio-cultural conditions, and economic as well as political factors (Haas and Schmitter, for example, establish their model of conditions by the examination of greatly differing international organizations: the EEC, EFTA, OECD, COMECON, West African Federation, Central American Common Market, East African Community, Latin American Free Trade Zone, etc.).[13]

Thus the explanatory value of the neofunctionalist models is still low. Even if they succeed in transcending somewhat the historicist mould that undergirds the historico-comparative list of conditions formulated by the Princeton group (especially, for example, in the case of Nye's propositions about integrative potential), one finds among them a mixture of morphological traits and determinants of various processes of regional international integration. In general, these models do not specify necessary and sufficient conditions but highlight, instead, conditions that are favorable to integration. Moreover, the major weakness of the neofunctionalist approach is to be found in its introverted analytic objectives as well as in its lack of attention to the phenomenon of externalization of the integrative process and its progressive and growing insertion into the international system. Neofunctionalism does not provide a sufficiently solid theoretical base for the projection of the regional integration process in general, and the process of European integration in particular, toward

---

[12]For a critical evaluation of the theory of European integration, see P. SOLDATOS, *Le système institutionnel et politique des Communautés européennes dans un monde en mutation,* Brussels, 1989, pp. 33–85.

[13]See, for example, their article, Economics and Differential Patterns of Political Integration, *loc. cit.*

the exterior, i.e., toward its environment and the relations with actors in that environment. It limits itself to acknowledging the presence of the externalization component of the process and it takes note of the presence of both hostile external actors and those favoring the process. Thus the need for a post-neofunctionalist approach to studying integration has become evident.

As for the European Community more specifically, this rather limited neofunctionalist attention to the process of externalization is easy to explain: a) neofunctionalism concentrates on the dialectic between nation state and supranational integration; b) its primary preoccupation is to circumscribe the internal dynamic of spillover towards political integration, and to do this from the perspective of a linear evolution toward the transcending of the nation state and the building of the United States of Europe; c) the originality of the Community integrative phenomenon, situated at the intersection of international organization and the state system, has attracted the attention of the neofunctionalists and induced them to concentrate on the internal process of the authoritative allocation of political values; d) from the fifties to the sixties, the neofunctionalist approach found itself facing a Community integration process conceived of as remedy for the functional incapacity of the nation state: its priority was from then on fixed on the step-by-step realization of internal integration; e) the international society of the fifties attempted to escape from the economic disintegration of the inter-war years and from the Second World War itself, and did not conceive of the structure of what is now called the world economy, which is most fruitfully investigated using a world systems approach.

The absence of an "integrated" model, representing the relations tying the European integrative system to the national subsystems, on the one hand, and to the global international system, on the other, constituted a major limitation in the theoretical approaches to European integration. It is indisputable that the regionally integrating systems played an important role for the functioning of, and for changes in, the international system. Therefore, an exact definition of the place of regional systems (in particular of the European system) in the circuit of interactions of the international system has yet to be developed. On the other hand, the relation in such a continuous circuit among the EC, the member states and member state subnational actors requires a systematic theoretical analysis from the perspective of interactions going beyond and within the nation state.

## III. THE CHAPTERS: AN OVERVIEW

It is quite evident by now that European integration is a complex human endeavor that has exercised the imagination and critical capacities of scholars in a large number of academic disciplines. In the chapters to follow are presented evaluations of some of the most important literature found in the five disciplines that have given the greatest attention to European integration: political science, sociology, economics, law and history. These chapters demonstrate that there are distinctive features in each discipline's treatment of the subject matter but also that there are numerous linkages across disciplinary borders, a finding that will not come as a surprise to anyone acquainted with the social sciences, humanities and law and, hence, with the high degree of overlap existing among them in their common quest to account for human behavior. Linkages across disciplinary boundaries are most clearly demonstrated in the work on European integration of such social science theorists as Ernst B. Haas, Karl W. Deutsch, Amitai Etzioni, Leon Lindberg and Joseph Nye, all of whom incorporated into their writing insights from cognate disciplines to make their arguments. Hence, it is not surprising that we find reference to the work of some of these authors in more than one chapter of this volume. There is, in particular, a good deal of overlap between the sociological and political science work on European integration, and the practitioners of the two disciplines tend, also, to borrow from the (more self-contained) disciplines of economics, law and history. In the case of political scientists, and to a lesser extent of sociologists, this can be explained in terms of their tendency to focus holistically on the overall process of European integration rather than to be content with narrowing their approach, like that of legal scholars and economists, to those aspects of human activity that their disciplines traditionally cover. Historians, while as broad in principle in their focus as political scientists and some of the sociologists, are not as likely as their social science colleagues to make an effort at grand theorizing, being more content to let "the facts" speak for themselves. This difference in the way in which the disciplines deal with European integration, viz., the tendency toward theorizing in the social science disciplines, on the one hand, and the more conrete, factual concerns of the legal and historical scholars, on the other, explains the subtitle of this book: "Theories and Approaches."

David Mutimer, a political scientist, focuses on the four approaches to European integration that have been most influential in his discipline. These approaches demonstrate rather well the sweeping generalizations that were attempted in the early literature, and also some of the disillusionment that set in when the actual course of events failed to reflect the expectations engendered by the theoretical literature. The first, and most explicitly political, approach to European integration is that of federalism. This approach is not *per se* a theory in the sense that it seeks to arrive at an understanding of the processes leading to the amalgamation of separate political units into one. Rather, it assumes the virtue of a particular, i.e., *federal*, arrangement of the institutionalized relationship among the integrating units and addresses itself to such issues as the division of powers between component units and the emerging central institutions. The strength of this approach is the clarity with respect to the goals of integration that it postulates; its shortcomings lie in its lack of specificity as to the process of arriving at these goals. Hence, while present-day advocates of a European Community with strong institutions still speak the language of federalism and encourage federalist goals, less enthusiastic Europeans or hostile opponents by their actions demonstrate the impediments to the attainment of such goals that federalist prescriptions have always faced.

The second theory Mutimer examines, functionalism (as most clearly exemplified by the work of David Mitrany), is very different from the federalist approach to international integration. Whilst federalists advocate explicitly political means to arrive at clearly political ends, Mitrany argues that such an approach is ill-informed in that it is unlikely to lead to a peaceful association of states, since the emphasis on political means and goals will lead to conflict and not peace. Hence integration should be depoliticized to the maximum extent possible both with respect to ends and means. International cooperation and the avoidance of conflict can and should be attained by focusing narrowly on welfare related issues and be unburdened of all attempts at forging comprehensive institutions fraught with implications for national sovereignty, questions of authority and, in general, highly emotive political concerns. However, as Mutimer shows, the assumption that a watertight separation between the political and the functional is possible proved not to be sustainable (for similar reasons that the Wilsonian insistence on the possibility of a distinction between politics and administration proved to be theoretically indefensible) and hence scholars, inspired in part by the ideological and theoretical reformulations of practitioners such as Jean Monnet, turned to what might be characterized as a synthesis of elements of federalism and functionalism.

The resulting synthesis, neofunctionalism, became the theory with most appeal to political scientists during the heyday of Euro-enthusiasm in the 1960s and 1970s. It led some of its proponents to expect an almost inevitable integration of the states participating in the three European Communities. The component mechanisms of the integration process (spillover, elite socialization, etc.) appeared to have as their logical consequences the creation of a strong set of central institutions and a gradual but almost inexorable transfer of sovereignty from member states to Community institutions. When this process lagged and then appeared to stall completely as a consequence of member state governments' reluctance about or even hostility regarding the loss of decision making powers, theorists reassessed the utility of neofunctionalism, and many abandoned it. But, as Mutimer argues in his chapter, it is possible, given the *relance* of Europe in the latter half of the 1980s and the early 1990s, to interpret the theory rather more sympathetically, and, given the role of Community institutions in the process leading to the Maastricht Treaty, to advocate a reassessment once the Treaty's fruits can be more fully evaluated. Hence, what has been viewed as a discredited theory may well have a *renaissance*, at least with respect to its ability to explain internal developments in the EC. Its failings with regard to the EC's role in the broader international context remains a critical weakness.

Mutimer concludes his treatment of political science theories and approaches with a discussion of Karl W. Deutsch's contributions to integration theory, his influential concept of security community. Deutsch's work, especially, exemplifies the interdisciplinary nature of the literature on integration theory because it is based on historical case studies, but also because it emphasizes concepts central to sociology and communications theory with their focus on shared meanings and social communication.

Werner J. Feld's chapter further examines this important sociological work on the creation of a sense of community among individuals in the political units moving toward integration. Central to this work is the emphasis on communication flows, the nature (balance or imbalance) in such transactions, and the socialization to new habits and values that favor the widespread identification with the integrating unit and thus sustain integration. Much of this work was done in the 1960s and 1970s, but the emphasis on values, attitudes and identification with the goals of European integration is carried on in the work of Ronald Inglehart and Jacques-René Rabier, as well as that of their collaborators and successors on the Eurobarometer project that continues to chart the degree of support among Community citizens for European integration and thus to remind us of the centrality of public opinion and human concerns for the integration process.

It is worth noting that much of what we have loosely referred to as the theoretical literature in political science and sociology was written during the early phases of European integration: the classics appeared in the late 1950s, during the sixties and in the early seventies. In subsequent years there has been a flood of empirical literature in political science and to a lesser extent in sociology, some of which we have referred to in earlier sections of this chapter. This literature has been most valuable in furthering our understanding of such topics as the Community's institutional development, its policies, the relationship between the Community and its member states, and the unfolding of relations between the Community and the world, but with the exception noted earlier about the tentative reassessment of neofunctional theory, there has not been a concomitant emphasis on the development of theory to explain the political and social processes involved. Whilst it would be unfair to call this literature totally a-theoretical or purely descriptive, it is, nonetheless, not characterized by a cumulative or integrated theoretical perspective. No doubt the earlier assessments about the failure of integration theory put a damper on high theorizing, but it appears fairly clear that such a hiatus in theorizing has not characterized the economics literature on European integration.

The chapter by Alfred Tovias provides strong evidence for the persistence of an emphasis in the economics literature on a step-wise expansion of the theoretical base that undergirds the economists' understanding of the Community, and economic integration generally. Explanations for this difference in emphasis among the social sciences would rest on a number of considerations including, probably, the following: the more strongly developed tradition in economics than in the other social sciences of basing academic work on explicitly stated theoretical postulates, the stronger emphasis on quantification and the need for conceptual rigor in applying this methodology and the more narrowly circumscribed phenomena that are typically the focus of economists' work. Hence, while political scientists and the grand theorists among sociologists tend to focus on whole systems and the explanation of a fairly broad spectrum of phenomena associated with European integration, economists typically address one or more phenomena that are more tractable and subject, more or less extensively, to empirical observation and confirmation.

As a further consequence, and even though the thoroughness of coverage of the topics relevant to European economic integration varies, there is, nonetheless, a steady development that leads to a higher degree of cumulativity and additivity in the economics literature on European integration than is the case for the literature in cognate social science disciplines. In that sense, as the chapter by Tovias demonstrates, theorizing on economic integration continues more systematically and more self-consciously than in the other disciplines. It is thus easier than in the other social sciences to show how various parts of the literature relate, and also to state what areas remain to be explored. It appears safe to conclude that the theoretical literature on economic integration will continue to make the steady progress that Tovias' survey demonstrates.

Alex J. Easson's chapter presents the legal perspective on European integration. It takes an approach that varies somewhat from that of the other authors in that it weaves into a substantive account of the major themes relevant to the Community legal order an account of some of the most significant literature dealing with these topics. Easson identifies the Court of Justice as the primary actor in the integration of Community law, itself probably the most important single instrument of European integration. He identifies the principles of direct effect and supremacy of Community law as key to understanding European legal integration, and outlines not only how these principles evolved, but also demonstrates their importance to the EC. In doing so, Easson provides a valuable account of law as an instrument and method of integrating Europe. He also treats the relationship between EC law and the European Convention of Human Rights, discusses the methods of applying Community law, outlines the role of law in the most significant recent Community developments and identifies the areas in which the Court will probably have to become active in the future. The balance of his chapter is dedicated to an examination of the relationship between the Court's role and that of the EC's non-judicial institutions, and on an evaluation of the merits and faults of judicial activism in the development of the Community.

Pierre-Henri Laurent provides us the insights of an historian about the literature on European integration. He argues that this literature can, from the perspective of the historian, be divided into that which deals with the founder years of the movement, i.e, from the end of the second world war until the establishment of the EEC in 1957/1958, and that dealing with subsequent developments. It is his contention that there is insufficient historical literature dealing with the latter period, and hence he examines the literature dealing with the first period.

Laurent outlines the major issues in the scholarly debate on the origin or causes of the integration phenomenon, identifying as some of these contentious issues among historians the respective role of external actors, the United States and the Soviet Union as well as the rivalry between them, on the one hand, and, on the other, more indigenous factors having to do with economic, political and strategic motivations of the European nations participating in the integration movement. In outlining the various positions on these issues, he introduces the reader to the major historical works on the early period of European integration and thus adds to a valuable short account of the origin of European integration an informative overview of the literature with which scholars wishing to explore the origins of the EC should be familiar.

In the pages that follow, then, the reader will be able to gain a comprehensive overview of the issues and perspectives that have motivated scholarly writing on European integration. The survey of theories and approaches demonstrates the richness of the literature on that phenomenon and the usefulness of using a multidisciplinary approach to explore it. The editors hope that the present volume may serve not only to outline the scholarly work that already exists, but also to motivate further research on what is one of the most important contemporary international developments, the movement toward greater unity in Europe.

# THEORIES OF POLITICAL INTEGRATION

David MUTIMER
*York University, Toronto*

In the Treaty of Rome the members of the European Community undertook to work toward achieving "an ever closer Union," an enterprise the Treaty of Maastricht is designed to fulfil. As it has been understood by the parties to those treaties, the members of the European Community, this enterprise is a commitment to creating an integrated political superstructure over the Community as a whole—in the language of students of European integration, a political structure at the supranational level. This begs the twin questions of how independent sovereign states come together to create a supranational politics, and what that supranational politics will look like once it is created. These are the questions that are at the heart of political theories of integration.

It is difficult to draw clear disciplinary boundaries under the best of circumstances, and the consideration of regional integration theory is not the best of circumstances for such divisions. Regional integration is a complex process which, when successful, involves changes across the social formations of the region: its economics, politics, law and society. Hence, theories of integration tend to span the conventional social science disciplines. Despite this broad compass to theories of regional integration, there is a distinctly political strand in this theorizing. At root, this commonality rests in the recognition of a common problem: the need to overcome war, particularly the need to prevent another in the series of wars that European nation states continued to fight. It is this fundamental concern with the construction of peace, and the central place that the nation state is seen to have in causing wars, that mark off political theories of integration. Underlying each of the approaches to regional integration which I will consider is a concern with building what Kant called "a perpetual peace," and an understanding that to build such a peace, we must move "beyond the nation-state."[1] Thus each of the theories seeks to describe and understand a process of integration among states which will yield *peaceful* political organization at a level above that of the national state.

---

[1]The term is the title of a leading study in the theory of integration, E.B. HAAS, *Beyond the Nation-State: Functionalism and International Organization*, Stanford, 1964. For a discussion of the roots of integration theory which draws the close connection with theories of international peace, see J. DE VREE, *Political Integration: The Formation of Theory and Its Problems*, The Hague, 1972.

In the present chapter, I will examine the leading theoretical approaches to political integration which have emerged from the study of developing peace in the drive to ever closer union. I will follow convention in suggesting that there are principally four such approaches: federalism, functionalism, its offspring neofunctionalism, and the communicative interactionism associated with the work of Karl Deutsch. As I examine each of these theories, I will be guided by the questions posed above: how does the theory under examination explain the dynamic of political integration, and what form of political union does it envisage emerging from the integrative process? The following presents a summary of the answers each theory gives to these questions.

**SUMMARY OF THEORIES OF POLITICAL INTEGRATION**

| | Integrative Dynamic | End Product |
|---|---|---|
| Federalism | Intergovernmental constitutional bargaining OR convention of a constituent assembly | Federal state |
| Functionalism | Establishment of successive functional organizations which drain the power from the national state | Collection of depoliticized functional organizations |
| Neofunctionalism | Spillover demands from integrated technical to increasingly political sectors | Institutionalized regional supra-nationalism |
| Communicative interactionism | Learning through communication, both at the social and bureaucratic levels. | Security Community |

To be useful, these theories must at least illuminate the practices of integration in Europe, and so I will conclude with some thoughts concerning the application of these theories to the recent *relance* of integration in the European Community. In doing so, I will suggest that these approaches to integration are best seen not as completing explanation, but rather as complementary accounts of the complex dynamics of the construction of supranational political community.

## I. FEDERALISM

As the League of Nations, based on sovereign equality and the principle of national self-determination, collapsed, scholarly and political attention turned to devising schemes whereby peace could be organized and secured. Particularly, once the League's failure led to a second world war, the question of how to organize international peace took on a special urgency. The leading answer to this question was the building of a world government, a central political authority which could police international violence in the same way that the state polices domestic violence. The most commonly proposed form of workable government was a federation of states. Proponents of federalism drew on the experience of and commentary on national federations, notably the United States, to suggest that the international community should come together and draft constitutions either for a global federation or for a series of regional federations.

The idea of a federal solution to the problem of post-war peace found particular appeal among the resistance movements on continental Europe. They blamed states and their sovereignty for the Second World War, and were determined to reshape Europe so that war would not recur. One of the earliest, and highest level, calls for a federal solution to the problem of post-war Europe came during the war when, in 1940, Winston Churchill called for a union of Britain and France. He had been advised in this by a group of British civil servants and French partisans in London—including Charles de Gaulle and Jean Monnet.[2] Following the war, and his electoral defeat, Churchill returned to the theme of European federal union, calling for the creation of a "United States of Europe" in a speech in Zurich in September of 1946. Churchill's seeming support for the idea of a federal Europe provided succor to the various groups of European federalists which had emerged from the resistance following the defeat of Germany. By May 5, 1949, they had succeeded in establishing the first European political organization, the Council of Europe, which it was hoped would usher in a new European federation.

The Council failed to achieve the dreams of its federalist founders—at least in part because of the opposition to federation of the British, including Winston Churchill once he returned to the prime ministership in 1951. In the meantime, however, a second integrative process was initiated, again under the lead of Jean Monnet. Monnet's "Community method" of integration was seen by federalists as a feasible alternative route to federation, given that the Council of Europe was not providing the direct route hoped. However, the Community method did not meet the expectations of the federalists either as, in 1954, the

---

[2]See E. WISTRICH, *After 1992: The United States of Europe*, London, 1991, pp. 22–23. The British had been working on a plan for a federal union of Britain and France and, in 1940, as Germany moved to consolidate its hold on France, Jean Monnet proposed the announcement by Britain of a potential union.

plan to create a European Defence Community was defeated in the French National Assembly. The defeat of the EDC also spelled the end for a parallel European Political Community, which would have established the foundations for a federal Europe. Following the defeat of the EDC, political thinkers and activists in Europe concerned with political integration divided between those favouring a gradual integrative project focussed on the European Coal and Steel Community and the later Communities of the Treaty of Rome, and those who felt that this route would never produce a politically integrated Europe. The first group has tended to be identified as neofunctionalists; the second continued to espouse federalism as Europe's political solution.

Federalism has the longest philosophical pedigree of any of the theories of political integration. One can find precursors to federalist thought in Ancient Greece and in medieval European political thinking, but federalism as it is commonly understood is an artifact of modernity. There are two principal sources of federalist thinking. The first is the profusion of peace plans from the seventeenth and eighteenth centuries in Europe.[3] These, as with the federalist plans which followed the Second World War, had as their aim the elimination of war in Europe, and involved some form of pan-European political organization. The most famous of these is Kant's *Thoughts on Perpetual Peace* (1795). The second source of federalist thinking is the American revolution or, more exactly, the American constitution. The American constitution is seen as the paradigmatic federalist arrangement, and the constituent assembly which gave rise to the constitution as the ideal means of achieving federation. Additionally, the debate over ratification of that constitution gave rise to the leading exposition and defence of the federal form of government, *The Federalist Papers*, of Alexander Hamilton, John Jay and James Madison.[4]

Once the United States was constituted as a federation, it served as a living model for the development of the ideas of federation. Study of the United States, along with other federal states as they emerged, served as an important source of federalist thinking. This comparative historical analysis also gives rise to an important critique of federalism as a theory of *international* integration. None of the cases of successful federation have, to date, involved the federating of established and functioning sovereign states. Rather, they involved joining recently emancipated colonies, or, in the case of Switzerland, small cantons with a very long history of political interaction.[5] It is thus a question as to whether

---

[3]For a discussion of these plans, see F.H. HINSLEY, *Power and the Pursuit of Peace*, Cambridge, 1963, particularly Part 1, pp. 13–149.

[4]Charles Pentland argues that there is a third source of federalist thinking, an amorphous body of thought concerning the small community, dating into the Middle Ages and finding its ultimate expression in Proudhon, although Rousseau also numbers in this tradition. See C. PENTLAND, *International Theory and European Integration*, London, 1973, pp. 158–161.

[5]The Swiss Confederation is considered to be over seven hundred years old.

federation on the American or Swiss model is appropriate for the political integration of established nation states, specifically whether it is feasible to federate the states of Europe. This, however, is precisely the federalist approach to international integration. As a theory of international (world or regional) integration, federalism seeks to apply the model of the federal state to the relations among nation states. To see precisely what this means, let me ask the two questions with which I began: what it the end product of integration, and what is the dynamic of the integrative process?

For federalism, moreso than for any of the other approaches to political integration, the end point of that integration is all important—much more important than the means used to achieve it. That end point, clearly, is the establishment of a federal state. As an approach to international integration, initially the hope was for a global federation in the place of the very loose United Nations. The tendency now is for proposals to be limited to regional federations, although with the goal of a global federation still firmly in mind. What then is meant by a federal state? Definitions vary, but the core of a federal organization of the state is the division of powers between two or more levels of government. R.W.G. Mackay has provided a definition of federalism in the context of a proposal for European integration:

> Federalism is a method of dividing powers of government so that the central and regional governments are within a limited sphere co-ordinate but independent. The test of the principles is: does it embody the division of powers between central and regional authorities, each being independent of the other? The principle is seen applied at its best in the United States of America, Australia, Canada and India.[6]

There is a necessary tension in the federal principle as a basis for political organization. While it can be seen as suggesting the creation of federal governments which join existing states, it can also be seen as a tool for the reform of states, suggesting the devolution of power within unitary states to regional authorities. Indeed, there is no theoretical limit to the number of devolutionary or integrative steps included in a federal organization. Extant federations function with two levels, a central government and state or provincial governments, but there is no reason, logically derived from a principle of federation, for such a limitation.[7] In the European context, this tension is

---

[6]R.W.G. MACKAY, *Towards a United States of Europe: An Analysis of Britain's Role in European Union*, London, Hutchinson, 1961, p. 83.

[7]This is not to say that more than two levels do not pose practical problems, especially in the context of a bi-level federation. Canada's recent experience illustrates this clearly. A 1992 constitutional proposal would have seen

manifest in proposals not only for a European federation, but also for the federal devolution of powers in unitary states, notably Britain. The possibility of a federation of federations has led to an important revision of federalist thinking in the European context. Ernest Wistrich has defined federalism in a recent proposal for a European Federation, and defined it in a manner that differs in important ways from the classical definition represented by Mackay: "The essence of federalism lies in the decentralization of power wherever needs can be satisfied at lower levels of government, closer to the citizen."[8] Wistrich's definition does not limit federalism to a two tiered organization of state power, the central and the regional, but captures in simple terms the multi-layered possibilities of federation.

This redefinition of the federal principle is of great importance in the contemporary movement to European Union. Decentralization wherever necessary is the principle of "subsidiarity," which is at the heart of the integrative program of the Maastricht Treaty. It should be clear that subsidiarity is not a violation, nor even a theoretical modification of federalism, but rather a recognition at the level of political practice of the logic inherent in the federal principle which has been hidden by the focus on extant, bi-level federations—principally the United States. Reginald Harrison has quoted French federalist Guy Héraud in a way that makes clear these connections:

> True federalism, [Héraud] says, is an extreme dilution and redistribution of power to give effect to different economic, social and cultural interests at many levels . . . "Le fédéralisme économique, social et culturel intégral dilue le pouvoir à l'extrême le répartissant entre tous les groupes et tous les hommes, et s'avère, de la sorte, dépolitificateur. Le fédéralisme reflète la dialectique de 'l'aplatissement' . . . toute philosophie qui tend à reduire la realité à un seul de ses élements constitutifs ou encore à une dimension unique . . . . Il s'agit de respecter la personnalité, les droits, les intérêts des collectivités de toutes sortes et de tous niveaux."[9]

Thus federalism, as it is being developed in the practice of European integration, holds out the promise of new form of state. A federation truly based on

---

the creation of a third level of government for Aboriginals, alongside the federal and provincial governments. The proposal was met with resistance not only from provincial governments who saw it as an encroachment on their powers, but also from Canadians at large, who saw it as "special treatment."

[8]E. WISTRICH, *op. cit.*, p. 2.

[9]R.J. HARRISON, *Europe in Question: Theories of Regional International Integration*, London, 1974, p. 46.

subsidiarity would not look much like any of our extant federations, as power would be diffused in varying ways and at varying levels throughout the union.

Federalism as an approach to European integration is centrally concerned with creating a federal Europe. Indeed, unlike the other theories considered below, federalism has largely been articulated by activists involved in the practices of European integrative politics.[10] This has tended to mean a greater focus on the end product of integration, the creation of federal institutions, than on understanding the dynamic of the integration process. Nonetheless, federalism does provide answers to this second question of the means of integration, although cast in the form of political strategy rather than social scientific analysis. Because of the importance of relatively specific constitutional forms to the federalist, the means for achieving integration necessarily involve drafting a written constitution of some type. The need for a constitution necessarily places intergovernmental bargaining at the heart of the integrative process, although two general routes to constitution making are identified by federalists.

The first approach to achieving federal integration is the constitutional convention. Modelled on the US experience, the argument is that a federal constitution should be drafted by popularly elected constituent assembly. The usual route proposed by federalists is that the constituent assembly will draft a treaty of union to serve as an initial federal constitution for Europe, which will then be adopted and implemented by the member states. The constituent assembly was the means chosen by the federalist movements in the early post-war period, and indeed the hope was that the Council of Europe would either act as or would create such a constituent assembly. Following the failure of the Council of Europe to produce a federation, federalists committed to this means of integration focussed their attention on the European Parliament.[11] They hoped to create a popular constituent assembly in stages, by having the EP elected by universal suffrage, which would then act to draft a Treaty of European Union. In this, the federalists were partially successful as the EP became an elected body in 1979, and before the end of its first session, it did produce the "Draft Treaty Establishing European Union." While this treaty was not adopted by the member states, it was central in promoting the process which led to the Single European Act and, ultimately, the Maastricht Treaty on European Union.

---

[10]Charles Pentland makes the case that there is a more academic strand of federalism, although its writers do not identify themselves as federalists. The leading writer Pentland identifies in this school, is Amitai Etzioni. Etzioni's work is considered elsewhere in this volume, along with other works of a sociological character. See C. PENTLAND, *op. cit.*, particularly pp. 151–155.

[11]The Parliamentary Assembly was renamed the European Parliament in 1979 in recognition of the status it gained from direct election. To avoid confusion with the federalist idea of a Constituent Assembly, I have referred to it as the European Parliament in both its incarnations.

The SEA and the Maastricht Treaty are clear examples of the second answer to the question of means. While some federalists remained committed to the constituent assembly model following the initial failure of the Council of Europe, others, notably Altiero Spinelli, adopted the Community means to a federalist end. In this second version of the federalist integrative process, the means of achieving federal union is by direct intergovernmental agreement. The creation of a federal state involves the member states ceding sovereignty to the central government, and so, the reasoning goes, it will only be achieved in an intergovernmental bargain. Federalists of this commitment focussed their attention on the Commission and the Council of Ministers rather than the Parliament; indeed, Spinelli became Technology Commissioner for the EEC.[12] The practical advantages of the intergovernmental method are amply illustrated by events of the 1980s. Both of the major advances in European integration, the Single European Act and the Maastricht Treaty on European Union were the result of intergovernmental conferences, as had been the original Treaty of Rome.

While the intergovernmental approach to federal integration has the advantage of addressing the question of state sovereignty, it shares with other federal approaches the problem of its not accounting for the *reasons* for states agreeing to federal union. Federalists argue that federation is the best answer to the problem of interstate violence, but there is a very long history of interstate violence that has not produced federation.[13] We are thus left to consider other theoretical approaches to international integration to see whether they are better able to provide insight into the conditions under which a process of intergovernmental bargaining will be entered, and in which an intergovernmental bargain on union may be successfully achieved.

---

[12]That Spinelli never lost his initial commitment to federalism is demonstrated by an even later intervention in the process. Spinelli was a leading member of the Crocodile Group of Members of the European Parliament which produced the Draft Treaty.

[13]The argument concerning federation as a guarantor of peace and security recreates the inherent tension, noted above, between domestic and international federation. Federation is supposed to guarantee peace by joining states together into a single political union—domesticating international conflict. This raises the question, however, of conflict between federal states and their neighbours. By federating a number of states, one creates a larger and more powerful whole, which is certainly more capable of waging wars than any of its consitituent units were before they were federated. The argument of the federalists, following in the tradition of Kant, is that democratic federations are less likely to engage in international violence than are unitary states—particularly between each other. I think it is safe to say that this argument remains unproven. For a discussion of this problem, see C. PENTLAND, *op. cit.*, pp. 166–174.

## II. FUNCTIONALISM

It was in the context of the imminent end to World War II with its need to reconstruct an international order shattered by the War, and against the backdrop of federalist proposals for a post-war world government that, in 1943, David Mitrany proposed an alternative method for international integration, what he called a "functional alternative."[14] In the first three pages of his pamphlet, *A Working Peace System*, Mitrany sets out "the general problem" as the need to form an "international government co-extensive with international activities." Given this problem, he argues, "A League would be too loose to be able to do it; a number of sectional federations would, on the contrary, be too tight to be welded into something like it; therefore, when the need is so great and pressing, we must have the vision to break away from traditional legalistic ideas and try some new way that might take us without violence towards that goal."[15] Functionalism was the break he proposed.

Mitrany was impressed by a number of arrangements which, nationally, bilaterally and internationally, had been developed along strictly functional lines, but which in the process had substantially altered what would traditionally be seen as the constitutional arrangements of states, without any formal constitution bargain. Of these examples, he seemed most affected by Roosevelt's New Deal in the United States:

> The significant point in that emergency action was that each and every problem was tackled as a practical issue in itself. No attempt was made to relate it to a general theory or system of government. Every function was left to generate others gradually, like the functional subdivision of organic cells; and in every case the appropriate authority was left to grow and develop out of actual performance. Yet the new functions and the new organs, taken together, have revolutionized the American political system.[16]

He contrasts this with a contemporaneous attempt to alter slightly the makeup of the US Supreme Court, which "was bitterly opposed and defeated," and yet

---

[14]D. MITRANY, *A Working Peace System: An Argument for the Functional Development of International Organization*, London, 1943.

[15]*Ibid.*, p. 7.

[16]*Ibid.*, pp. 21–22. In addition to the American New Deal, he also notes a series of working arrangements between Canada and the United States which were developed during the war, fewer but similar efforts among the North Americans and the British, and, notably, the International Labour Organization which survived the demise of the League of Nations.

which involved a less substantive change to American government than the functional arrangements of the New Deal.[17] To Mitrany, the conclusion for international relations was obvious. If the United States, an extant federation with a tradition of the peaceful settlement of constitutional disputes, could not even make minor adjustments to its constitutional arrangements, what were the chances of a collection of sovereign states voluntarily ceding their sovereignty to a newly created international federation? Thus, if the failed and tortuous constitutional route did not provide a solution, what of the pragmatic, functional approach of the Tennessee Valley Authority?

> Instead of keeping up the old and barren attempt to establish a formal and fixed division of sovereignty and power, a division which changing conditions continually puts out of joint, we could with a little insight and boldness distribute power in accordance with the practical requirements of every function and object. Instead, that is, of asking *by whom* should sovereignty and power be exercised, we should rather ask *upon what* objects they should be exercised; or, to put it in other words, the real question is not "who are the rightful authorities," but rather "what are the rightful ends—and what are the proper means for them?"

This, in a nutshell, is Mitrany's functional alternative. Rather than gathering states together to develop a blueprint for political union, states would build particular authorities to administer the provision of relatively narrowly defined services. It is these various services which are the rightful ends he speaks of above, and the particular form of each administration is to be determined by the proper means to provide them. In order to understand more clearly what Mitrany had in mind, and how his functionalism was to serve as a means of political integration for the preservation of peace, it is useful to pose of it the two questions with which I began. First of all, what is the dynamic of the integration process?

To functionalism, the key dynamic for integration is the transnational nature of international problems. Provision of railway or airline transportation, to use two of Mitrany's examples, requires organization across international frontiers. Similarly, this same travel has brought new diseases which require action at the international rather than the national level. Even the economy, the bulwark of the nation state, needs an organizing hand beyond the reach of that state—as the Great Depression had proved so clearly when Mitrany first started

[17]*Ibid.*, p. 22.

to write of his functional alternative.[18] These transnational problems create a demand for transnational solutions, just as the economic problems of the Great Depression created a demand for the sorts of economic intervention of Roosevelt's New Deal. Just as Roosevelt responded with functional organs, regardless of the location of constitutional authority, so too should states respond to the demands of these transnational problems by creating functional agencies to resolve them.

At this point, some of the problems with Mitrany's functionalism as a *theory* of integration begin to emerge, problems similar to those confronted by federalism. *A Working Peace System* was clearly intended as a normative document, setting out an agenda for change. The pamphlet thus does not make clear the relationship between the demand for international services and their supply in functional organizations.[19] It could be read to imply a functional explanation:[20] that is, that the supply of functional organs at the international level is *explained* by the need for them in transnational problems. A more reasonable reading is that the construction of a functional system is a policy choice open to states when faced with transnational problems. If this is the case, however, Mitrany seems to be back to the point he was trying to escape: states gathering to construct a global system to which they will cede sovereignty. To see how he both tries to avoid this conclusion, and how he is ultimately unsuccessful, it is necessary to be clear about what Mitrany envisages to be the end point of this integrative process: what is functional integration?

Mitrany provides a simple answer to this question as he begins to outline his program:

> What would be the broad lines of such a functional organization of international activities? The essential principle is that activities would be selected specifically and organized

---

[18] While *A Working Peace System* is the most complete expression of Mitrany's functionalist thinking, the outlines of the idea can be found in his 1933 work, *The Progress of International Government*.

[19] I borrow here Robert Keohane's language on the problem of international regimes. It is an appropriate parallel, since the regime literature grew in the 1970s as a response to the seeming demise of regional integration as a result of the same international pressures: the need for international cooperation in conditions of state sovereignty. See R. KEOHANE, The Demand for International Regimes, in S. KRASNER (ed.), *International Regimes*, Ithaca, 1983, pp. 141–171.

[20] The overlap in terminology is unfortunate, but unavoidable. It should by now be clear that Mitrany's theory is referred to as functionalism because of the centrality of organizations focused on the provision of *functions*. Functionalist explanation, by contrast, *explains* features of social life exclusively with reference to the function that they serve. There is thus no necessity that a functionalist theory of integration will employ functional logic.

> separately, each according to its nature, to the conditions under which it has to operate, and to the needs of the moment. It would allow, therefore, all freedom for practical variation in the organization of the several functions, as well as in the working of a particular function as needs and conditions alter.[21]

Organizations would thus be devised to address needs in particular areas of activity, and organized so as best to address these needs. However, this allows us only to rephrase, not to answer, the problem of supply. How would these activities be selected, and once selected, how would they be organized? At this point, Mitrany reveals himself a functionalist, in both senses of that term, by proposing a solution based in functional reasoning:

> Here we discover a cardinal virtue of the functional method—what one might call the virtue of technical self-determination. The functional *dimensions*, as we have seen, determine themselves. In a like manner, the function determines its appropriate *organs*. It also reveals through practice the nature of the action required under the given conditions, and in that way the *powers* needed by the respective authority. The function, one might say, determines the executive instrument suitable for its proper activity, and by the same process provides a need for the reform of that instrument at every stage.[22]

The activities, therefore, are self-selected, and the functions to be provided in turn determine the way in which they are provided and the structure and powers of the organization. It still seems unclear how even this technical decision making process (or abdication of decision making, as might be more appropriate) is to overcome state sovereignty. It is in his answer to this problem that the final form of Mitrany's functionalism begins to emerge:

> All students and most political spokesmen are insisting that the states must be ready to surrender some of their sovereignty, but is there any prospect that we could secure acceptance for a new view of formal sovereignty, and so of state equality? But the content and working of sovereignty could be modified by such inconspicuous and partial transfers of authority to international functional organs more effectively, just because

---

[21] D. MITRANY, *op. cit., pp. 32–33.*

[22] *Ibid.*, p. 35.

> they would leave untouched a fundamental principle which the smaller states, who are the many, cherish as the bulwark of their independence. . . . In other words, that most disruptive and intractable of international principles, the principle of state equality, may well be tamed by specific functional arrangements which would not steal the crown of sovereignty while they would promise something for the purse of necessity.[23]

States would, in other words, be tricked into ceding their sovereignty by having it emptied of meaning. States would agree to the functional arrangements because they promised to provide services which the states require, but the formal title of sovereignty would not be transferred to an overarching federation. The heart of this trick is an understanding of politics which clearly divides the political from the technical, so that functions can be depoliticized and, hence, not a concern to the political authority, the state:

> *Any* political scheme would start a disputation; *any* working arrangement would raise a hope and make for confidence and patience. The functional way may seem a spiritless solution —and so it is, in the sense that it detaches from the spirit the things which are of the body. No advantage has accrued to any one when economic and other social activities are wedded to fascist or communist or other political ideologies; their progeny has always been confusion and conflict. Let these things appear quite starkly for what they are, practical household tasks, and it will be more difficult to make them into the household idols of "national interest" and "national honour."[24]

Thus the end of the integrative process Mitrany envisioned was a technical administration of international society, organized into units based upon the provision of functions. This might ultimately grow into a world federation of some form (he does allow for the possibility), but it is neither inevitable nor necessary. States would thus be emptied of the political power and identity which had led to conflict, and instead of its being recreated at a higher level, the very idea of political division—defined, it seems, as ideological and territorial—

[23]*Ibid.*, p. 29.

[24]*Ibid.*, p. 56.

would be replaced with a technical association: an international civil service providing for the needs of the world's people.[25]

It is on this rigid division of the political from the technical that the functionalist theory has received its greatest criticism. As Reginald Harrison has pointed out in a critique of integration theories, most, if not all, "functional" services ultimately involve the allocation of resources, and such allocative decisions are necessarily political.[26] There are other deficiencies in functionalist theory, which have led to its largely being abandoned as either an analytic or normative approach to international organization.[27] However, some of the central ideas of Mitrany's system have been reformulated into one of the most important of the theories of integration, called, in the fashion of political science, neofunctionalism.

## III. NEOFUNCTIONALISM

If functionalism is seen as the work of David Mitrany, the neofunctionalism is principally identified with Ernst B. Haas, although it is also identified with the work of Haas' student, Leon Lindberg, and with Amitai Etzioni.[28] Haas began with a critique of Mitrany's functionalism, and then through a pair of important studies of integrative organizations, developed a theory of integration which differs from its functionalist predecessor both in its conception of politics, and in the scope of its application.[29] Haas rejected

---

[25]*Ibid.*, pp. 39–41. Mitrany explicitly calls for the creation of an international civil service, as opposed to a "mass of national groups." Such a service would develop an internationalist ethos, which Mitrany argues would serve as a guarantee against the sorts of divisive ideologies which have been associated with the states system.

[26]R.J. HARRISON, *op. cit.*, pp. 32–36. Harrison notes, for example, that the state of Massachusetts took the federal government to court over federal appropriation of monies to reduce maternal and infant mortality, because Massachusetts was a net contributor to federal allocative resources. This is an established federation with, supposedly, fellow feeling among "Americans."

[27]For a discussion of the problems with functionalism, see *ibid.*, pp. 27–39, and C. PENTLAND, *op. cit.*, pp. 64–87.

[28]For reasons of brevity and focus, I will concentrate on the work of Haas, particularly as Etzioni's contribution to integration is addressed in another chapter of this volume. Lindberg's principal contribution to neofunctionalism in the tradition of Haas is a study of the European Economic Community using the framework Haas had established to consider the Coal and Steel Community. See L. LINDBERG, *The Political Dynamics of European Economic Integration*, Stanford, 1963.

[29]In the two texts which form the initial statements of the neofunctionalist approach to integration, Haas studies first the European Coal and Steel Community, and then the International Labour Organization—although in the latter, he explicitly

Mitrany's assumption that a reasonably clear split could be made between the political and the functional, allowing for the "emptying" of the nation state's political power by means of the creation of functional institutions at the international level. This led Haas to a theory of *political* integration at the international level. In large measure because of this, he also considered that the preconditions among the states to be integrated were more stringent than Mitrany required. Thus he proposed *regional* integration in place of Mitrany's universal international integration.

The fundamental critique of functionalism, which gave rise to Haas' neofunctionalist position, is that of the separation of the political from the economic. In *Beyond the Nation-State*, Haas clearly states this criticism:

> Power and welfare are far from separable. Indeed, commitment to welfare activities arises only within the confines of purely political decisions, which are made largely on the basis of power consideration. Specific functional contexts cannot be separated from general concerns. Overall economic decisions must be made before any one functional sector can be expected to show the kind of integrative evolution that the Functionalist describes. . . . The distinction between the political and the technical, between the politician and the expert, simply does not hold because issues were made technical by a prior political decision.[30]



---

disavows that his text is a case study of the ILO. See, respectively, E. HAAS, *The Uniting of Europe: Political, Social and Economic Forces, 1950–57*, Stanford, 1958, and E.B. HAAS, *Beyond the Nation-State, op. cit.*

[30] E.B. HAAS, *Beyond the Nation-State, op. cit.*, p. 23. The argument that neofunctionalism differs from functionalism on the basis of a recognition of the relation between politics and economics is an important and oft-stated one. Given this importance, I feel that it is essential to make the case as strongly as possible. Haas, and others, use a number of different words to refer to both the political and the economic in discussing this relationship, and so it is important to draw the connections between, for example, *politics* and *power*, and between *economics, welfare* and *technique*. Let me, therefore, quote extensively from *Beyond the Nation-State*, in which Haas set out the functionalist position, making use of the various terms to refer to the political and the economic:

(1) The Functionalist separates power from welfare. Both are thought of as representing types of human and state aims; great insistence is placed upon the distinction, and a great many programmatic points follow from it.

(2) The Functionalist further separates various governmental tasks into discrete elements, even if only temporarily. But he insists on completely separating military-defense (power-oriented) task [sic] from economic-abundance (welfare-oriented) tasks, in addition to isolating various kinds of welfare tasks. . . .

His critique of functionalism notwithstanding, Haas does see that Mitrany is onto something by attempting to divide the political from the functional:

> Yet the proposition does clarify a point confused by realists who wish to subsume all of international relations to the search for national military security. Organization programs tied to the totality of all aspects of all national foreign policies never seem to enjoy implementation, whereas well-defined narrow programs conforming to parts of policies or certain states fare much better.[31]

The economic is thus not entirely separable from the political, as Mitrany would have us believe, but there is still a distinction on which a process of political integration can be built. As Haas writes elsewhere, "[t]he history of the European Union movement suggests that the relationship between politics and economics remains somewhat elusive."[32] It is precisely the elusive nature of the relationship between the economic, or technical, and the political upon which neofunctionalism is built as a theory of political integration.

The link between the critique of functionalism and the development of a neofunctionalist theory of integration raises the first of the two questions I pose of each approach: how does it explain the dynamic of integration? The answer of the neofunctionalist is that integration can be understood as a response to the pressures created by "spillover."[33] Haas introduces the notion of spillover in his discussion of the development of the ECSC in *The Uniting of Europe*:

> Thus a "spillover" into new economic and political sectors certainly occurred in terms of expectations developing purely in the *national* contexts of the elites involved. Yet these expectations were reinforced along supranational lines not only

---

> (3) A still finer separation occurs in the crucial distinction between the political and the technical, the work of the politician and that of the expert. [*Beyond the Nation-State*, p. 21].

It is thus clear that Haas sees the functionalist position as delineating a clear separation between the political, whose ambit is that of power and the politician, and the economic, whose ambit is that of welfare and the technician.

[31] *Ibid.*, p. 47.

[32] E.B. HAAS, The Uniting of Europe and the Uniting of Latin America, *Journal of Common Market Studies*, vol. 5, no. 4 (1967), p. 315.

[33] For the following discussion of spillover I draw extensively on my article, 1992 and the Political Integration of Europe: Neofunctionalism Reconsidered, *Journal of European Integration*, vol. 13, no. 1 (1989), pp. 75–101.

> because action was demanded of the High Authority but because continuous joint lobbying with labour leaders from other countries became both necessary and possible.[34]

Reginald Harrison has succinctly characterized the nature of spillover:

> This is the "expansive logic of integration," otherwise called the "spillover" effect, whereby "policies made pursuant to an initial task and grant of power can be made real only if the task itself is expanded, as reflected in the compromises among the states interested in the task." The acceptance of each stage in this integration process "is best explained by the convergence of demands within and among the nations concerned, not by a pattern of identical demands and hopes."[35]

Spillover assumes that the various elements of the political economy of states and regions are interconnected in such a way that problems in one area will raise problems or require solutions in another. In this way, the expectation is that when certain economic functions are placed in the hands of central bodies, a demand for increased power at the centre will result from the need to look beyond the originally integrated area for solutions. As Harrison noted, these solutions do not require the complete agreement of states, but rather a general convergence of similar interests around the goals of the *original* common undertaking. This suggests that decisions with spillover implications may be reached, even in the face of fairly substantial division among states.

At the outset, it is assumed that such spillover will occur only among different functional tasks, but that as the centre grows, more politically salient areas will begin to be affected. Harrison has discussed the effect of the spillover logic for the growth of political integration:

> Ultimately, the expectation is that as the tasks and powers of the central institutions are increased through the operation of the spillover process, integration will gradually encroach on that politically sensitive area where vital interests are at stake. So, an embryonic political community will emerge and grow.[36]

---

[34]E.B. HAAS, *The Uniting of Europe, op. cit.*, p. 292.

[35]R.J. HARRISON, *op. cit.*, pp. 76–77.

[36]*Ibid.*

Political spillover is thus the necessary result of the move to reconnect the economic and the political in the way Haas did. Economic or technical tasks must be conceived as sufficiently distinct that they can usefully be integrated separately, but not so much so that once removed to the supranational level the issues have no more connection to the competencies remaining with the nation states. Given this conception of a partial separability between economic and political tasks, it is assumed that economic integration will gradually accelerate, spilling over incrementally into larger and larger areas, encroaching further and further into the political sphere, until a "takeoff" point is reached. After the takeoff point, the central institutions will spill over at a dramatically increased rate, and community building will begin in earnest.[37]

An important shift in neofunctionalist thinking has eliminated much of the determinism that was originally included in this formulation of spillover.[38] Primarily as a result of the problems the EEC confronted in the late 1960s, integration came to be seen as a probabilistic, rather than a deterministic, outcome. On this view, the probability of spillover increases as the salience of the issue involved increases to the community at large. In addition, to the degree that automaticity is eliminated from the spillover logic, it allows for the inclusion of the all important element of political will. Regardless of the pressures for increased centralization within the community, the position of the member states is still sufficiently strong that substantial transfers of authority will depend upon the will of the governments involved.[39] This form of integration becomes self-reinforcing at this point, because central institutions, once they are formed, can act to facilitate intergovernmental agreement—to build and shepherd member states' political will into greater integrative action. This mechanism is aptly demonstrated in the recent *relance* of the European Community.

If neofunctionalism explains integration by means of spillover within an "elusive" matrix of politics and economics, how does it address the second question, that of the end product of integration: what will neofunctionalist integration produce? In a review of his work in integration, Haas answered this question in the negative: "The verbally defined single terminal conditions with

---

[37]The takeoff point is not particularly well defined, either analytically or empirically. It derives, it would seem, from a belief in the inevitability of spillover, and the fact that human institutions do develop a momentum which can lead to periods of exponential growth once substantive obstacles are cleared. For a discussion, see *ibid.*, pp. 79–80.

[38]J. De Vree has suggested that the process was seen, by Haas at least, as nearly inevitable, with expansion of decision-making competencies driving the demand for further expansion, seemingly *ad infinitum*. See J. DE VREE, *op. cit.*, pp. 126–127.

[39]C. PENTLAND, *op. cit., p. 100.*

which we worked in the past—political community, security community, political union, federal union—are inadequate because they foreclose real-life possibilities."[40] In other words, neofunctionalist theory does not specify a particular end point to integration, and does not do so by choice. Rather, it conceives of integration as a *process*, and allows for an open ended product, a procedural solution. However, while the end product is ill defined, it is clearly intended to be institutional. As Jane Sweeny has written in a recent attempt to assess neofunctionalism in relation to the development of the European Parliament, "institutions are an important *outcome* of the integration process, that is, they are a measure of the success of the integration project."[41] It is on the question of the form these institutions will take that neofunctionalism makes no firm commitment. Integrated neofunctionalist institutions involve the exercise of parts of states' sovereignty "beyond the national state," but without these powers fully being relinquished to an autonomous institution. Rather, the integration process involves giving "greater powers and competence to common organizations, and [increasing] the range and importance of the decisions taken jointly rather than separately by national governments."[42]

In order to discuss this conception of integration, neofunctionalism introduces the idea of "supranationality," often called the "pooling" of state sovereignty, as opposed to its transfer. The sovereign authority of a state is extended to the supranational authority, where it is pooled with that of its fellow member states. The spillover process suggests that more and more of the states' sovereignty will be pooled in this manner, but the precise institutional form of the supranational authority is left undefined. This being said, neofunctionalism would seem to privilege federal institutions as the end point of integration. Federal solutions are privileged because federation has tended to be the manner in which independent units have historically been joined. For this reason, people see the pooling of sovereignty at the supranational level as a prelude to federation—particularly given the salience of a potential federal state in the leading example of international integration, the European Community. However, while neofunctionalist integration can lead to a federal state, it can also give rise to integrated structures short of a supranational state, or to a state of a nonfederal character. Neofunctionalism is not theoretically limited to any particular level or kind of political integration.

---

[40]E.B. HAAS, The Study of Regional Integration: Reflections on the Joy and Anguish of Pretheorizing, *International Organization*, vol. 24, no. 3 (1970), p. 631.

[41]J. SWEENY, *The First European Elections: Neofunctionalism and the European Parliament*, Boulder, 1984, p. 25.

[42]C. PENTLAND, *op. cit.*, p. 100.

One reason that the creation of a supranational state is an expected outcome of neofunctionalist integration is that the spillover mechanism does not only operate at the level of the state elites, but is to be expected at the mass level as well. As functional integration generates greater and greater demands on supranational authorities which, in turn, take on ever greater competencies, the political demands and eventually identifications of the *people* of the member states may be expected to spillover as well. As Haas writes in *Beyond the Nation-State*: "Personal political loyalties are the result of satisfaction with the performance of crucial functions by an agency of government. Since actors can be loyal to several agencies simultaneously, a gradual transfer of loyalties to international organizations performing most of the crucial functions is likely."[43] Such a spillover of political loyalties, however, is limited in important ways. Haas argues that the conditions for such a spillover are exacting, and that "the introduction of these qualifications tends to eliminate from the sweep of the proposition all the world's totalitarian nations, as well as those nations of Asia, Africa, and Latin America in which oligarchies now rule peoples rapidly being mobilized and clamoring to participate in politics. . . ."[44] Indeed, Haas generally qualifies the applicability of neofunctionalist integration by arguing not only that it is possible solely among states which are organized under liberal democratic constitutions, but also, because of the tight links among economies needed for the spillover mechanism to work, it requires relatively advanced industrial societies. Neofunctionalism is thus a theory of *regional* political integration, rather than a universal theory as was Mitrany's functionalism.

The recognition of the regionalism inherent in Haas' formulation of neofunctionalist integration allows me to specify it a little more clearly. Neofunctionalism describes integration among a regional grouping of liberal democratic states with advanced economies, by means of functional and political spillover, and towards the greater institutionalization of decision making in a supranational authority. Such a characterization identifies neofunctionalist integration as defined principally as *process*, rather than with reference to a particular *product*. It also seems to conjure a strong image of the European Community. The connection between neofunctionalist theory and European Community practice is sufficiently strong that a fair presentation of the former must at least address its relationship to the latter.

In a book length review of the theories of political integration, Charles Pentland has characterized neofunctionalism as "the European Community method of integration." As he makes clear, the relationship between neofunctionalist theory and European Community practice is a complex and uncertain one:

---

[43]E.B. HAAS, *Beyond the Nation-State*, *op. cit.*, pp. 49–50.

[44]*Ibid.*, p. 50.

> In many respects the relationship between the European Community and neofunctionalist ideas would make a fascinating study in the sociology of knowledge. Works such as those of Haas and Lindberg, based on interviews and personal contacts in the Community environment, and on massive absorption of Community documents, inevitably imbibe the ethos and assumptions of those organizations and become in a sense, their academic expression. The reverse relationship is rather more elusive—Monnet, Hallstein, Spaak and their successors being first and foremost pragmatists—but it can be assumed at least that the extensive theorizing carried on about the Community's workings has served to reinforce what rapidly became the "conventional wisdom" of Brussels.[45]

Seen in this light, neofunctionalism becomes less a general theory of regional integration, but rather a conceptualization of the drive to "an ever closer Union" in Western Europe. This imbues neofunctionalism with a strong normative commitment to the integration of the European Community, despite its presentation of itself as positive theory. Neofunctionalism can thus be seen both as a theoretical description of the way in which the European Community is developing as an integrative project, and as a "manual" for the integration of Europe—and of anywhere else that wishes to follow the same method. Such a conclusion would offend the behaviouralist sensibilities of the original neofunctionalists, but I think that in a time in which behaviouralism, and positivism more generally, is coming under attack in international relations, it is not an unreasonable one.

Neofunctionalism thus provides relatively rigorous formulation of the means of political integration developed *ad hoc* by Jean Monnet and his colleagues in the 1950s. In addition, it provides for the wide dissemination of these ideas in a form which provides them with the added legitimacy of academic science. In this way, neofunctionalism both describes and constitutes the political integration of Europe. Nevertheless, despite its close connection with the most successful current example of international integration, neofunctionalism does not stand unchallenged as *the* theory of political integration, and indeed to understand the context of neofunctionalism, it is necessary to understand not only the functionalism from which it grew, but the competing theories which were drafted alongside it, of which federalism is only one.

---

[45]C. PENTLAND, *op. cit.*, p. 132. The chapter on neofunctionalism in Pentland's book is entitled: Neofunctionalism and the European Community Method of Integration.

## IV. THE IDEA OF SECURITY COMMUNITY

The final stream of thinking on political integration is that primarily associated with the work of Karl Deutsch. Deutsch's theory of political integration, which I will label communicative interactionism, illustrates superbly the problem of drawing disciplinary boundaries. As the following introduction to his work makes clear, Deutsch mined disciplines other than political science for the conceptual tools he would use to understand political integration:

> Deutsch's work can best be understood in the light of [the] relatively early state of scientific development [in political science]—as one great attempt to develop a new language of politics. In doing so, he does not feel himself bound to political science as delimited traditionally or to any one of its more or less current conceptual schemes. On the contrary, he consciously explores other fields and disciplines in search of schemes and lines of reasoning which might be applied in political science. . . . Thus, intertwined with purely political considerations or detailed historical narration, we meet with highly abstract cybernetic or communication-theoretical reasoning, and with general sociological analyses in which sometimes a Parsonian terminology is used.[46]

For this reason, Deutsch's work is considered in more detail elsewhere in this volume together with other approaches which derive from academic sociology. However, a survey of approaches to political integration would be incomplete without some consideration of Deutsch's work, particularly the idea of a security community.

For Deutsch, the dynamic of integration is found in the learning of individuals in social groups—groups he classes as communities, societies and cultures. The social groups are defined primarily with reference to interaction, although clearly simple interaction is insufficient to create meaningful social groups. Thus to form a social group, the collection of interacting individuals must partake in stable structures of communication: a community is "a group of persons who are able to communicate information to each other effectively over a wide range of topics."[47] Learning, in turn, is driven by this communicative interaction; it is the developing of increased capacity to communicate in the process of communicating. Such increased capacity to

---

[46]J. DE VREE, *op. cit.*, pp. 167–168.

[47]K.W. DEUTSCH, The Growth of Nations: Some Recurrent Patterns of Political and Social Integration, *World Politics*, vol. 5, no. 2 (1953), p. 169.

communicate builds and strengthens community, a process of building which is Deutsch's concept of integration. For Deutsch, then, integration is a process of community building as learning, driven by communicative interaction among people at both the mass and elite levels. It is from this emphasis on communicative transaction flows that the notable empirical research of this approach derives: the attempts made to measure communication by examining, for example, data on mail flows, telephone calls and tourism.

Of more continuing interest to theorists of political integration than Deutsch's understanding of the integrative process were some of his ideas concerning the nature of the political community to which integration would give rise. Particularly, the idea of a "security community" has proven to be one of considerable intellectual currency:

> A *security community* is a group of people which has become "integrated."
>
> By *integration* we mean the attainment within a territory of a "sense of community" and of institutions and practices strong enough and widespread enough to assure, for a "long time," dependable expectations of "peaceful change" among its populations.
>
> By *sense of community* we mean a belief on the part of individuals in a group that they have come to agreement on at least this one point: that common social problems must and can be resolved by processes of "peaceful change."
>
> By *peaceful change* we mean the resolution of social problems, normally by institutionalized procedures, without resort to large-scale physical force.[48]

The form which the "security community" can take is even less clearly specified in Deutsch's work than is the form of institutionalized supranationalism in Haas'. Indeed, Deutsch outlines three types of "security community," depending on the degree to which political institutions have been developed across that community. The security community can range from the "no war community," which satisfies only the minimal requirements of an expectation of peaceful

---

[48]K.W. DEUTSCH *et al.*, *Political Community and the North Atlantic Area: International Organization in the Light of Historical Experience*, Princeton, 1968, p. 5. This is a formal presentation of the definition Deutsch uses in his *Political Community at the International Level: Problems of Measurement and Definition*, Garden City, NY, 1954, p. 33. While it is from Deutsch's work that this concept of security community has come into the literature on integration, and his usage is universally cited as the reference point, the initial formulation of the definition of security community is found in R. VAN WAGENEN, *Research in the International Organization Field: Some Notes and a Possible Focus*, Princeton, 1952, pp. 10–11. In both works on political community Deutsch quotes Van Wagenen.

change, through a "pluralistic community," in which there are but a few central political institutions, to an "amalgamated community," in which central institutions are established across the community area.[49] Thus where most theorists of European integration examine the European Community for their case support, Deutsch argues that a pluralistic security community is in evidence among the states of the North Atlantic area.[50]

It is the development among this broad range of centralized political institutions which is the central concern of the other theorists of political integration. Thus the entire scope of what a federalist or neofunctionalist would consider as integration is conceived by Deutsch as fine tuning of an already integrated whole. However, the idea of a "security community" as a precursor to neofunctionalist or federalist integration is very appealing, as it points to an all-important condition for political integration: what Deutsch calls a "sense of community." Without a sense among the people of an area, both at the mass and elite levels, of common belonging, it is impossible to conceive of the sort of transfer of political legitimacy which is central to the neofunctionalist conception of political spillover. Without the general expectation of "peaceful change," institutionalization of either a neofunctionalist or federalist kind is similarly inconceivable. Thus Deutsch's work suggests the need for examining questions of political sociology in order to complete the theoretical account of political integration. Whether or not the particulars of Deutsch's communicative interactionism are accepted, there is a clear need to account for the development of communal identities among the people of integrating areas if we are to understand political integration to include the legitimation of the emergent central institutions.[51]

## V. INTEGRATION THEORY AND THE EUROPEAN *RELANCE*: TOWARDS A SYNTHESIS

Theorizing political integration is closely related to the practice of that integration, principally in Europe. The approaches that I have detailed above all grew and suffered along with the institutions of European integration. Thus, most of the work that I have considered here was written in the 1950s and 1960s.

---

[49]K.W. DEUTSCH, *Political Community at the International Level, op. cit.*, pp. 34–44.

[50]K.W. DEUTSCH *et al.*, *Political Community and the North Atlantic Area.* In their conclusions, the authors argue that Canada, the United States, Ireland and Great Britain may form the nucleus of an *amalgamated* North Atlantic community!

[51]The question of identity formation is very much a current concern in a stream of sociological literature far removed from Deutsch's Parsonian concerns. See, particularly, A. GIDDENS, *Modernity and Self-Identity: Self and Society in the Late Modern Age*, Cambridge, 1991.

In the 1970s, the European Community seemed to have stalled, and regional integration theory was renounced as "obsolescent" by its leading figure, Ernst B. Haas.[52] With this intellectual recantation, students of international cooperation moved away from theorizing political integration to the nascent theory of international regimes. However, the European project has not proven to be moribund, and so it seems necessary to ask what place the theory I have been discussing has now that the European Community is moving again towards its "ever closer Union."

In a work that in part attempts to answer this question, Robert Keohane and Stanley Hoffmann have recently argued that the failure of theories of integration, notably neofunctionalism, to predict the *relance* of the mid-1980s requires us to rethink integration theory: "What was unpredicted by analysts working with established theories cannot, in general, be adequately explained post hoc through the use of such theories."[53] They proceed, along with Andrew Moravcsik in the chapter following theirs, to critique the accepted theories of integration and call for new thinking to account for the *relance*. Both of these works suggest that to account for the Single European Act, integration theory must begin with intergovernmental bargains.[54] Keohane and Hoffmann argue that these intergovernmental bargains, based on a convergence of interests among the leading states of the Community, are the fundamental explanation of the SEA, although spillover of the neofunctionalist kind and pressures from the international political economy were also important.[55] Moravcsik argues that to understand the form of the SEA, one needs to examine the bargaining among the national leaders, and that those bargains are explicable in terms of convergent national interests.

The conclusions reached by these authors suggest that the old theories of political integration cannot simply be resurrected, but it would seem that there

---

[52]The term is from E.B. HAAS, The Obsolescence of Regional Integration Theory, Research Series No. 25, Institute of International Studies, University of California, Berkeley, 1975. On Haas' views on the end of regional integration theory, see also E.B. HAAS, Turbulent Fields and the Theory of Regional Integration, *International Organization*, vol. 30, no. 2 (1976).

[53]R. KEOHANE and S. HOFFMANN, Institutional Change in the 1980s, in R. KEOHANE and S. HOFFMANN, eds., *The New European Community: Decision Making and Institutional Change*, Boulder, 1991, p. 3.

[54]See *ibid*., particularly pp. 10–17, and A. MORAVCSIK, Negotiating the Single European Act, in R. KEOHANE and S. HOFFMANN (eds.), *op. cit*., pp. 46–48 and pp. 64–75. The chapter is reprinted from Negotiating the Single European Act: National Interests and Conventional Statecraft in the European Community, *International Organization*, vol. 45, no. 1 (1991), pp. 651–688.

[55]R. KEOHANE and S. HOFFMANN, *loc. cit*., Institutional Change, pp. 10–25.

is insight to be gleaned from applying the core ideas of these theories to the new integrative projects—perhaps more than either article allows. Neither Keohane and Hoffmann nor Moravcsik accept that the European Parliament is particularly important in explaining the move to the Single European Act. However, the "Draft Treaty Establishing European Union," while it was not adopted by the member states, did initiate the process that led to the SEA. Moravcsik notes that "[o]ne of the Dooge Committee's first actions was to reject the European Parliament's "Draft Treaty Establishing European Union" and begin negotiations with a French government draft instead.[56] But that the Dooge Committee was struck at all is only comprehensible in the context of the Parliament's tabling of the Draft Treaty. Thus it is the Parliament's Draft Treaty that allows us to understand the *timing* of the *relance*, a timing which, as Keohane and Hoffmann note, is central to understanding the *relance* as a whole.

I want to highlight the importance of the Draft Treaty, because once it is recognized, then part of Keohane and Hoffmann's objection to the traditional theories disappears even on their own terms of its failure to predict the events of the 1980s. Consider the following discussion of the Federalist political agenda, published in 1974:

> [A] number of stages of federalist progress were envisaged. First, the activity of the European Economic Community and of Parliament, with supporting propaganda from federalists, will draw the attention and interest, and probably the support, of industry, commerce and agriculture to the goal of European Unity. The second stage would be to secure the election of the European Parliament by direct suffrage. The European parliamentary assembly would then become the potential instrument of the next stage of progress, acting as a permanent, though non-sovereign, constituent assembly. . . . The final stage would be the conclusion and campaign for the ratification of a Treaty drafted by the Assembly and, thereafter, the creation of the necessary institutions envisaged by the Treaty.[57]

Now compare this predicted process to that followed by the European Community *following* the publication of Harrison's text. In 1979 the European Parliament was elected by direct universal suffrage. In 1984 the Parliament proposed its "Draft Treaty Establishing European Union," as foreseen in the second and third stages of the federalist project. While this Treaty was not

---

[56]A. MORAVCSIK, *loc. cit.*, p. 64.

[57]R.J. HARRISON, *op. cit.*, p. 49.

adopted, it initiated a process which led directly to the Single European Act, and then to the Treaty of Maastricht which, if ratified, will create a European Union.

There is another problem with the focus on intergovernmental bargains which can, in part, be addressed by an appeal to elements of the old integration theories. The convergence of interests which give rise to intergovernmental bargains may explain why those bargains are useful, but it does not necessarily explain why they are achieved. This is the same problem confronted by the federalists in their reliance on intergovernmental bargaining. In Keohane's language, which I cited above, convergent interests allow us to understand the demand for integration, but not necessarily the supply. There are a number of examples of convergent state interests which can best be satisfied by cooperative and coordinated action—indeed the literature on international regimes is built on these examples. How is it that these convergent interests can be translated into integration in Europe, and not in other parts of the world? Here it is possible to appeal to the existence of supranational organs committed to the completion of the integrative project. Even Moravcsik, who wants to deny that supranational (i.e., European Commission) action is central to explaining the SEA, notes that "[t]he approach proposed here . . . accords an important role to supranational institutions in cementing existing interstate bargains as the foundation for renewed integration."[58] That is, the intervention of the Community organs serves to facilitate the translation of convergent interests into integrative action.

It would seem that these authors labour hard largely to recreate Haas' notion of non-deterministic spillover. The development of convergent interests can be thought of in terms of the generation of spillover pressures. Mutual involvement in common enterprises will shape problems in common, giving rise to common interests in achieving solutions. These spillover pressures are not necessarily converted into greater integration, rather it is contingent on gaining actor agreement—this is the essential move in eliminating determinism. For neofunctionalists, supranational institutions then play an important role in facilitating that agreement. Given the ephemeral nature of governmental agreements, such a facilitating mechanism cannot be ignored in an account of renewed integration.[59]

---

[58] A. MORAVCSIK, *loc. cit.*, p. 75.

[59] Moravcsik concedes that "the remarkable speed of the [intergovernmental] conference might be attributed, at least in part, to the role of Delors and the Commission in proposing and revising the specific wording of treaty amendments. While logistical support from the Commission may indeed have hastened a final agreement, there is little evidence that it altered its substance" (p. 66). If the importance of speed for translating political agreement into constitutional change is in doubt, a review of the Canadian experience with the 1989 Meech Lake Accord should prove enlightening. Over a two year ratification process, a unanimous agreement among eleven governments eroded and the package of amendments failed. The supporters of the Maastricht Treaty would also, I suspect, wax eloquent in favour of measures to speed passage of agreements.

Finally, one of the reasons that both sets of authors have found intergovernmental bargaining to be of such central importance is that their focus was limited to the Single European Act itself. If the renewed integrative project is considered broadly, and the focus is on more than simply the specific treaty amendments of the 1987 Act, both federalism and neofunctionalism appear in a more favourable light. I have elsewhere examined the process of completing the internal market begun by the SEA, with an eye to the political implications of that process and through the lens of neofunctionalism. What I found was that the neofunctionalist concepts, particularly those of spillover and of institutionalization, were revealing of the way in which the 1992 project unfolded, both leading up to the passage of the SEA and afterwards. Indeed, based on that examination I predicted the further *political* integration before the call of the second round of intergovernmental conferences in 1989 which led to the Treaty of Maastricht.[60]

Thus, while Keohane, Hoffmann and Moravcsik may be right that political integration needs renewed theorizing in light of the *relance* in Europe in the 1980s, it is possible that a synthetic approach that builds on the lessons of the earlier theorizing will be a useful way to proceed. Federalism and neofunctionalism certainly provide insight into the process by which the Community reached the point where renewal of integration was seen as a necessary response to international conditions and convergent interests. The supranational institutionality of the EC, of central importance to Neofunctionalist theory, played an important role in the speed with which the SEA was negotiated, a speed which was a key to its success. Spillover is evident in the development of convergent state interests, in the manner by which the single market completion proceeded, and in the second phase of the *relance* leading to the Maastricht Treaty on European Union. Finally, the negotiation of that Treaty was infused with the ideas of federalism, as federalists used the negotiations to push for a federal Europe, while their opponents worked specifically to avoid an outcome labelled "federal." The one important area of omission in these theories, that Moravcsik rightly points to, is the domestic politics of the member states. Any synthetic theory of European integration must account for the role played by domestic politics, particularly given the democratic nature of the European polities. Even here the old theories provide some guidance, as Deutsch's communicative interactionism indicated the importance of developments at the mass level for the growth of political community.

The call for a synthetic renewal of integration theory, particularly one which begins with Keohane and Hoffmann's critique of that theory for its failure to predict the *relance*, begs the question of what theory is and what it is useful

---

[60]See D. MUTIMER, *loc. cit.*, pp. 95–100.

for. While I am not here to conduct a study of the philosophy of science, a few words on this question are in order, and I will begin with Keohane and Hoffmann's own words, in a note to the passage on prediction quoted above:

> The present authors doubt whether any theory that can perfectly predict strategic behavior of states will ever be devised. Unconstrained strategic behavior is inherently unpredictable insofar as optimal action changes depending on each party's perception of the expectations of others. Theory, if widely known and accepted, creates expectations, which provide incentives for actors to devise strategies exploiting those who have such (now conventional) expectations—*thus invalidating the theory.*[61]

If we accept that predictability is not a reasonable evaluative criteria for integration (or other social scientific) theory, then why is it that failure to predict renders theory invalid? Perhaps the inevitability of modification of actor behaviour, rather than invalidating theory, changes the nature of that theory and our expectations about it. The three political theories of integration I have reviewed, federalism and the two forms of functionalism, were all proposed in part—indeed in large part—as programs of political action. Even neofunctionalism was both an account and a codification of a practically developed theory of action. Indeed, as Keohane and Hoffmann rightly note, Haas never conceived of the central dynamic of spillover as a deterministic process—and some measure of determinism is necessary for accurate prediction.[62]

An attempt to recover theories of political integration in this manner is not to say that some form of rethinking is not necessary—indeed it is essential—as the theories were put forward as predictive theories of political behaviour. However, if these theories form part of the understandings of the political actors in Europe who are making the key decisions leading to integration, then they cannot simply be abandoned. Rather, they must be rethought on the basis of a non-deterministic, interpretive philosophy of science—in the words of a recent discussion of theory in international relations, a philosophy aimed at "understanding" rather than "explaining."[63] Such a reformulation is well beyond

---

[61] R. KEOHANE and S. HOFFMANN, *loc. cit.*, notes 6, 34 (emphasis added).

[62] In the physical sciences, the decline—some would say the outright rejection—of determinism has resulted from two theoretical developments which radically undermine predictability: quantum mechanics and chaos theory. On the death of determinism, see P. DAVIES and J. GRIBBIN, *The Matter Myth*, New York, 1993, particularly pp. 10–63.

[63] M. HOLLIS and S. SMITH, *Explaining and Understanding in International Relations*, Oxford, 1991.

the scope of this chapter, but it suggests a very different approach to achieving a synthetic theory of integration than that of Keohane and Hoffmann and of Moravscik.

## VI. CONCLUSION

Following a decade of dynamism and excitement in Europe, there is the fear of a renewed Europessimism. For proponents of integration, the Treaty of Maastricht seemed a weak compromise when it was reached in December of 1991, and the difficulty that it is having being ratified does not bode well for the creation of an "ever closer Union." It is important, however, not to draw too many long term conclusions from short term observations. European integration was considered dead in the water in the 1970s, and barely ten years later the European Community was being hailed as the new superpower for the twenty-first century. Clearly, abandoning integration and integration theory just because the Community is experiencing a pause or even a setback on its road to integration is an over-reaction. The disillusionment of the 1970s can perhaps be explained by a faulty philosophy of science. If one expects to predict social behaviour in the way the physicist predicts the behaviour of a simple pendulum, then disappointment is inevitable. However, if we recognize that integration is indeterminate, and that theories of integration, more than explaining an objective process, in part constitute the understandings of the actors involved in political integration, then we have a basis on which to renew the study of political integration.

# SOCIOLOGICAL THEORIES OF EUROPEAN INTEGRATION

Werner J. FELD
*University of Colorado, Colorado Springs*

This essay is concerned with sociological explanations of European integration. From a sociological perspective, society is seen as being in a process of evolution and progress; what is to be determined are the uniformities governing this process and the meaning of integration. Karl Deutsch has defined integration as "the attainment, within a territory, of a 'sense of community' and of institutions and practices strong enough and widespread enough to assure, for a 'long' time, dependable expectations of 'peaceful change' among its population."[1] A sense of community exists when individuals in a group of people agree that social problems must and can be resolved through institutionalized procedures without resort to large scale physical force.[2]

The integration process in which Western Europe was mostly involved began in 1953 when the European Coal and Steel Community, encompassing six member states, entered into force. In 1993 the number of member states has risen to twelve, and all economic sectors in the European Community (EC) territory are included in the integration process. To carry out all the needed tasks for the member governments, the EC has required expanded and more sophisticated facilities and organization.

Considering the current accomplishments of the Community, two questions must be asked and, hopefully, answered within the theoretical limits of this essay: 1) what have been the factors and variables leading to the current state of integration, and 2) what will be the prospects for future integration, especially with respect to political unification? As Amitai Etzioni has written, sociology can contribute to this kind of study since in international relations ideology has now become "a major force, nonrational ties among nations [are] more common, institutional bridges . . . more numerous." Thus, international relations have become more amenable to sociological analysis. Of these trends,

---

[1]K.W. DEUTSCH, *Political Community and the North Atlantic Area*, Princeton, 1957, p. 5.

[2]*Ibid.*

teresting to the sociologist is the formation of new unions nations (e.g., the European Economic Community).[3]

## AL UNIFICATION

The notion of political unification followed by the establishment of a political community was part of Etzioni's theorizing in the 1960s and 1970s. The unification process is one in which control of the means of violence, the capacity to allocate resources and rewards, and the locus of identifications are transferred from member units to the system in which they are members. It may well be that the degree to which these units are *internally* integrated may affect their potential resistance to unification and, therefore, the success of any specific unification efforts.[4]

To move the unification process forward requires integrating power. Etzioni distinguishes between coercive, utilitarian, and identive power.[5] This classification covers both "real" (coercive and utilitarian) and "ideal" elements. It represents those major sociological schools: the Italian school of Pareto and Mosca which was especially concerned with force; the Marxist school; and the Weber-Durkheim tradition which emphasized sentiments and ideas.[6]

While coercive power may not be relevant in examining the potential unification process of the European Community at this stage, the application of utilitarian and identitive power may contribute to its progress. Indeed, the economic *effects* of "1992" may strengthen the identitive potentials which, according to Etzioni, consist usually of values or symbols, "built up by educational and religious institutions, national rituals, and other mechanisms."[7] Of course, instead of national rituals, supranational or regional rituals would be more appropriate in the EC case in order to produce the required changes in the relations among and within the member states to keep the unification process moving. As Etzioni points out, such changes tend to be resisted by some of the member states or subunits involved in the process or by outsiders whose utilitarian interests and identitive commitments may motivate them to support the maintenance of the status quo.[8]

---

[3] A. ETZIONI, The Epigenis of Political Unification, in A. ETZIONI and E. ETZIONI, *Social Change*, New York, 1964, p. 481.

[4] A. ETZIONI, *Political Unification*, New York, 1965, p. 16.

[5] *Ibid.*, p. 37.

[6] *Ibid.*, p. 38.

[7] *Ibid.*

[8] *Ibid.*, pp. 41–42.

There are other variables which Etzioni considers important to explain the unification process. One variable is the degree of elitism among the initiators and supporters of this process. Is the leadership interested in unification endorsed with greater political, economic, and identitive power than the opponents of unification? Do the proponents enjoy a concentration of power within the system considered for unification, in this case, the EC, and how widely are the beliefs and objectives of the elite distributed among the general public? How far have the elites emerging from the member units or the EC institutions taken over the control of the system, a process referred to as "internalization of power"?[9]

Another major variable examined by Etzioni relating to the unification process is the communication capacity of a unit involved in this process. "The effectiveness of the communication network of a unit or system affects the degree to which its assets can be converted into actual power."[10] Effective communication, however, requires not only the transmission of information but also certain qualities and processes within the receiving units. Obviously, if a decision making unit is overloaded with communications, is ideologically rigid, or for some other reason is not able to digest the communications received, the clarity and effectiveness of the message will be seriously undermined.[11] While there can be little doubt about the instrumental value of communications for the process of unification, the substance of the message remains decisive with regard to the progress of unification and the EC system will be no exception.

Finally, Etzioni seeks to determine when unification is terminated. He recognizes that unification may not be completed and that regional cooperation systems such as the EC may and in fact do integrate only gradually, depending on the breadth and scope of the decision making powers which have been transferred to the central institutions by the constituent treaty and actual practice. He also hypothesizes that the more integrated a community is, the more unit autonomy it can tolerate. In turn, the strength of unification is determined by the "dominant function" which is served by the collectivity and it is this function, according to which the unifying communities "invest more resources, manpower, energy, and which they value more highly as compared to other communities."[12]

There is little doubt about the dominant function of the European Community, but it will require considerable empirical research with respect to the elitism, internalization, and communications variables to assess the

[9] *Ibid.*, pp. 45–50.

[10] *Ibid.*, p. 43.

[11] For more details on this subject, see K.W. DEUTSCH, *op. cit.*, p. 12.

[12] ETZIONI, *op. cit.*, p. 62.

identitive and utilitarian assets in order to come to conclusions regarding the status of the EC unification process at present and in the future. But Etzioni's concepts appear to be promising and furnish a valuable judgment on a highly political subject.

## II. COMMUNICATIONS AND TRANSACTIONS

We have touched on the instrument of communications as a significant variable in Etzioni's theoretical framework of the political unification process. But the content of communications as well as the transactional nature of communications between nations and societies have stimulated additional and complementary theoretical thought to explain regional integration and unification of cooperating nation states. Karl Deutsch's seminal mind is to be credited with the concepts on communication theory and transaction flows relating to political integration that follow.

Focusing upon transactions and other forms of social communications, Deutsch considers various transactions as the first step toward estimating the degree to which people are connected with each other. The second step in measuring this degree can be determined by the study of covariance, which refers to the study of joint rewards and penalties. Deutsch contends that the actual probability of a joint reward may be called "interest" in the objective sense. The concentration of attention upon an expected joint reward or deprivation would be the subjective aspect of the problem. The classic learning theory describes what happens when there are many rewarding transactions in a community. When there are many joint rewards, the people who have experienced these mutual transactions will like them.[13] When these transactions are highly visible, easy to identify and differentiate, people may form images of the community or group involved in the transactions. If these transactions were rewarded, the image of the community may be strongly positive. Liking this kind of community, people may say, "We belong together." In their favorable reaction to the community, they might then also say, "I can see myself as a member of this community"; "I will call it 'we' if I speak of a group. I will call it 'home' if I speak of a territory."[14]

From the above set of assumptions, Deutsch postulates two hypotheses. First, if people have experienced a high level of transactions, with substantial joint rewards at one time, they may be willing to accept joint deprivations at a later time, provided joint rewards come again still later. Second, a group of people taught to identify with each other by means of initial

---

[13]K.W. DEUTSCH, Communication Theory and Political Integration, in P.E. JACOB and J.V. TOSCANO, *The Integration of Political Communities*, Philadelphia, 1964, p. 54.

[14]*Ibid.*

joint rewards but then reinforced by a probalistic mixture of joint rewards and joint deprivations will show greater cohesion and greater strength of habit than a group of people who have experienced nothing but joint rewards. Moreover, rewards must come before the penalties and rewards must be strong and frequent to initiate the habit.[15] The rewards, perceptions and responses can be measured through sampling attitudes and they may be able to be confirmed through the study of group behavior and voting behavior.

Deutsch has proposed to use selected transaction flows as quantitative indications of social communications and has sought to apply statistical and content analyses regarding mail flow, telephone traffic and other measurable transactions such as tourism, migration, imports and exports, and transnational currency transfers.[16]

Donald Puchala has attempted to explore the strengths and limitations of transaction analysis and has concluded after a very careful examination that transaction flows provide reasonably reliable descriptive barometers for several social, economic, and political processes that occur during regional integration.[17] The term "transaction" applies, of course, to a very large number of phenomena and activities in the relations among cooperating nation states and, in order to contribute insight and order to transaction analysis, the construction of indices is a necessity. The most concise measure of intensity of transaction flow standardized for relative "size" of transacting units appears to be the "relative acceptance transformation index." It standardizes for "size," reduces cumbersome absolute figures to decimal indices, and measures such factors as transaction intensity (high relative acceptance [RA] scores in some channels, low ones in others), partnership or interdependence (high RA scores in both directions in bilateral channels), and dependence (high RA scores in one direction only). RA scores can show both communication links and communication gaps between actors and, since the index relates either to total world or regional transaction universes, they can capture specific bilateral or multilateral shifts in transaction behavior.[18] From his extensive inquiry Puchala concludes that while transaction flows *reflect* and describe regional integration, they do not explain it. In other words, "transaction flows do not *cause* regional integration."[19] There is then some risk in using transaction analysis

---

[15]*Ibid.*, p. 55.

[16]K.W. DEUTSCH, Transaction Flows as Indicators of Political Cohesion, in P.E. JACOB and V. TOSCANO, *op. cit.*, pp. 75–97.

[17]See D. PUCHALA, International Transactions and Regional Integration, *International Organization*, vol. 24 (1970), pp. 732–763.

[18]*Ibid.*, p. 738.

[19]*Ibid.*, p. 762.

"predictively" in integration studies. According to Puchala, this type of analysis cannot as yet contribute to answering causal questions.

Bruce M. Russett seems to agree with Puchala that transaction flows do not *cause* political integration in the sense of being a sufficient condition. But Russett believes that institutionalization must occur if transactions *remain* at a high level. Otherwise, either the flow of transactions may have to be reduced or the needed institutions have to be constructed.[20] But Russett also insists that transaction data do not predict institutionalization nor do they make it possible as a necessary condition for integration.[21]

In addition to being high relative to other systems, Russett contends that transnational transactions within the system under consideration for integration must be *balanced*, truly an exchange, and that this balance is perceived as such by the citizens. Finally, the transactions must be high relative to loads or burdens and be seen as "capabilities" for the participating units.[22]

## III. THE LEARNING OF INTEGRATIVE HABITS AND THE INFLUENCE OF VALUES

Basic concepts of learning theory are at the base of Henry Teune's social science theories and his variables concerning political integration between nation states. He applies the term "political integration" to two general categories of behavior: (a) when certain stimuli are responded to in roughly the same way by a significant number (possibly a majority) of people, and (b) when collectivities of people respond to each other as relevant stimuli; moreover, the adult segments of the population may teach these response patterns to their children, to reward other members of the collectivity for responding in the same way, and to punish deviations.[23]

As for specific categories of variables relating to political integration, Teune selects *inter alia* the "spillover" theory of political integration,[24] primarily involving two principles of learning theory, that of frequency of association and that of generalization of stimuli; the "rational" calculation of payoffs for political integration; and shared values and expectations in political integration.

---

[20]B.M. RUSSETT, Transactions, Community and International Political Integration, *Journal of Common Market Studies*, vol. 9 (1971), pp. 224–245.

[21]*Ibid.*, p. 235.

[22]*Ibid.*, pp. 239–240.

[23]H. TEUNE, The Learning of Integrative Habits, in P.E. JACOB and V. TOSCANO, *op. cit.*, p. 257.

[24]See E.B. HAAS, *The Uniting of Europe*, Stanford, 1958, pp. 283–317.

Teune states that cooperation, alliances, and mergers between political communities—instances of political integration—can be explained as the result of rational calculation of payoffs and rewards. Of course, there will be wide individual differences in the impact which changes in rewards can have on changes in beliefs and behavior.[25]

As to shared values and expectations, a persistent hypothesis concerning political integration is that shared or mutual values and value systems ease the way for greater political integration. Teune contends that viewed from the perspective of "stimulus-response" learning theory, shared values reflect similarity in conditioning, and similarity in conditioning facilitates a mutual transfer of stimuli or symbols. If all nations were paired on the basis of similarity of what is valued, then this hypothesis would predict that greater political integration in terms of tariff agreements, treaties, shared decision making institutions, and avoidance of war should obtain among the more similar nations.[26]

Political identification is another focus of Teune's learning theory since, according to him, such an identification is a "learned drive."[27] If a substantial portion of a population living within a political boundary has learned that political identification is rewarding or has a learned pattern to be politically identified with a specific set of political stimuli, then this collectivity of people could be called a political community.[28] How far the potential rewards of "1992" may be the stimuli to affect current and future political identifications with Europe is a most interesting question and makes learning theory a top candidate for further empirical inquiry.

The influence of values in political integration is also examined by another scholar, Philip E. Jacob. He is primarily concerned with the values of decision makers and with the decision procedures that may influence the integration process at the policy level and the overall Community level. The major focus is on the decision maker's "personality as it emerges through his socialization, the specific expectation which people around him have of what he should do in the social roles he occupies, and the characteristic behavioral patterns of the culture of which he is part. . . . His decision is affected not only by what he desires but by yardsticks which define for him what is right or wrong, praiseworthy or blameworthy . . . these criteria . . . we identify as 'values.'"[29]

---

[25]H. TEUNE, *op. cit.*, p. 262.

[26]*Ibid.*, p. 264.

[27]*Ibid.*, p. 270.

[28]*Ibid.*, pp. 270–271.

[29]P.E. JACOB, The Influence of Values in Political Integration, in P.E. JACOB and V. TOSCANO, *op. cit.*, p. 211.

Jacob points out that in order to be successful with integrating a larger community, leaders holding a deviant set of values at first may have to effect the breakdown of the existing political orders based on norms which seemed to have become anachronistic and needed to be replaced. The value deviators would be those leaders and people who considered themselves as "Europeans" while the remainder would remain committed to Spain, France, Greece, and the other member states. But Jacob also warns that historically there is no "inevitable" progression from smaller to larger political communities.[30]

## IV. POLITICAL CULTURE

For Claude Ake,[31] the problem of political integration is essentially one of developing a political culture and of inducing commitment to it. For him, political culture consists of the system of empirical beliefs, expressive symbols and values which defines the situation in which political action takes place. For the political system as a whole, it provides a systematic structure of values and rational considerations which ensures coherence in the performance of organizations.[32]

Ake is *not* focusing on the events and developments in the European Community. His interest is national integration mostly in Third World countries and political integration is understood to be part of it.[33] Nevertheless, some of the thoughts of Ake may be useful for understanding the process of integration among developed nation states in Western Europe as well and, therefore, those appearing to have relevance are briefly covered.

Ake states that a political system is integrated when individual units develop in the course of political interaction a pool of commonly accepted norms regarding political behavior and a commitment to the political behavior patterns legitimized by these norms. Commitment to these norms channels the flow of exchanges (outputs and inputs, actions and reactions, expectations and responses) among interacting political actors and units. In effect, it gives coherence and predictability to political life.[34]

The nature of the values which constitute the political culture must be such that commitment to them furthers the persistence of the political structure. Moreover, one important element in the political culture is the individual's

---

[30] *Ibid.*, p. 245.

[31] C. AKE, *A Theory of Political Integration*, Homewood, Ill., 1967.

[32] *Ibid.*, pp. 1–2.

[33] *Ibid.*, pp. 12–14.

[34] *Ibid.*, pp. 3–4.

belief about the ultimate focus of his political identity. Taking together all the considerations articulated by Ake, it seems that their acceptance and pursuit may, in due time, strengthen the momentum of the EC political integration process. Most likely political culture may be one of a number of variables to explain the European integration process; indeed, it is one that should not be overlooked.

## V. GENERATIONAL VALUE CHANGES

An extensive study of the values of Western publics with major emphasis on the European Community countries, undertaken by Ronald Inglehart, has suggested that a major shift of values has taken place, producing "a decline in the legitimacy of hierarchical authority, patriotism, religion, and so on, which leads to declining confidence in institutions."[35] The causes of the value changes are economic and technological development with satisfaction of sustenance needs for expanding proportions of population, distinctive cohort experiences as the result of absence of "total" war during the past generation, rising levels of education, and expansion of mass communications with increases in geographic mobility. Hence, according to Inglehart, there has been an increasing emphasis on needs for belonging, esteem, and self-realization, with increasing salience of "life style" issues, relative decline in social class conflict, and the rise of supranational and "tribal" loyalties.[36]

Among the many forces for change are economic development, expansion of secondary and higher education, the growing size and diversity of the mass media and discontinuities in the life experiences of large numbers of people. Inglehart argues that, apparently, "nationalistic sentiments are not being transmitted to the young with the same fidelity as in the past. Governments traditionally have exploited patriotic symbols as sources of legitimacy for their actions. As popular support of these symbols declines, governments can no longer draw so easily on this source."[37]

One result of this change could be an increased openness to international integration. But the search for social identity can also move in the opposite direction. There has been a resurgence of demands for autonomy based on language and culture in Belgium, France and Great Britain. Thus, we may face a relative emphasis on both supranational and subnational ties that may exist in the same individual.[38]

---

[35]R. INGLEHART, *The Silent Revolution*, Princeton, 1977, p. 4.

[36]*Ibid.*, p. 5.

[37]*Ibid.*, p. 14.

[38]*Ibid.*, p. 15.

Inglehart points to two significant phenomena to explain the change in values: a) the unprecedented prosperity experienced by Western nations during the decades following World War II, and b) the absence of total war. The simple fact that no Western nation has been invaded for over four decades may have extremely significant consequences. "In short, people are safe and they have enough to eat. These two facts have far-reaching consequences."[39]

As society may have been changing from traditional industrial society to post-industrial society, value definitions became subject to shifts from "materialist" to "post-materialist." Inglehart hypothesized that those who had been socialized under conditions of peace and relative prosperity would be most likely to have post-materialist values. He also assumed that materialists consistently gave a higher priority to national prestige.[40] Moreover, public opinion surveys within the European Community countries in the early 1970s bore out Inglehart's predictions that the old would be more likely to have materialist value priorities than the young; conversely, the post-materialist type should be more prevalent among the young.[41]

The analysis of the surveys regarding the value priorities offer some insights into the prospects of European political unification. Inglehart concludes the following based on his findings. Traditionally, the nation state has based its claims to legitimacy, in large part, on its function in preserving domestic order and protecting its subjects from foreign enemies. Evoking real or imagined threats to national security has been a perennial means to rally public support for the existing regime. The military establishment still retains a positive public image, but the *priority* accorded to national defense seems to have fallen to a remarkably low level among Western publics. One of the key symbols of nationalism may have lost much of its potency, and a further shift toward post-materialist values would imply a further weakening of support for the nation state.[42]

While there are indications that a society characterized by a large number of post-materialist value preferences would provide better conditions for the political integration of the European Community, progress toward such an outcome would depend on the development of an appropriate ideology and on the number of people in the member states who would commit themselves to such an ideology. But according to Inglehart, no one has yet proposed a truly coherent and socially acceptable ideology for a post-industrial society.[43]

---

[39]*Ibid.*, pp. 21–22.

[40]*Ibid.*, p. 28.

[41]*Ibid.* See pp. 31–39 for details. In a 1972–73 survey, Belgium had the highest ratio of post-materialists to materialists (.56) and Denmark the lowest (.17).

[42]*Ibid.*, p. 70.

[43]*Ibid.*, p. 372.

Nevertheless, even without an appropriate supportive ideology, Inglehart's findings indicate that the relatively prosperous post-materialists now comprise the most likely source of political dissatisfaction and protest and that they show more support for radical change than materialists.[44] Hence, they may represent a public eager to push the unification process forward.

Another favorable aspect of political integration prospects is the rising level of political skills which would enable Western publics to play a more meaningful role in the decision making process. According to Inglehart, there is evidence from a number of countries that the influence of the political machine, labor unions, and the church may be eroding gradually. Hence, the Western publics may be approaching a threshold at which they can take part in actual decision making rather than entrust it to relatively skilled, elite-directed minorities. Those publics, based on survey data in the early 1970s, seem to be gradually taking on a sense of supranational identity,[45] and if this trend has continued and will continue, it may provide a favorable outlook for unification. During the surveys conducted for Inglehart's book, it was only among the young that the post-materialists came close to equalling the materialists in numbers. But by the end of this century, it was anticipated that the post-materialists might constitute a large share of the population of Western nations, and that they would be concentrated among the most active and influential sectors of the society.[46]

Although Inglehart's basic concepts of postmaterialism/materialism and generational shifts remain intact in the 1980s, survey data collected in the middle of the decade indicate that in the expanded Community of the Twelve, European unification no longer has the appeal for youth (and postmaterialists) which it possessed one or two decades earlier. The tendency for the young to be relatively pro-European continues, but the tendency has weakened, and the polarity in two of the newer member states—Denmark and Greece—is reversed.[47] Moreover, those espousing postmaterialist values and who were expected to be the strongest supporters of European unification have declined in their support from 1970 to 1986, while the support of the materialists, although dropping as well during this period, was only about half of that of the postmaterialists in the first place and by 1984–86 showed only a nine point spread compared to the latter.[48]

---

[44]*Ibid.*, p. 367.

[45]*Ibid.*, p. 368.

[46]*Ibid.*, p. 383.

[47]See R. INGLEHART, J.-R. RABIER, and K. REIF, The Evolution of Public Attitudes Toward European Integration: 1970–1986, *Journal of European Integration*, vol. X, nos. 2–3 (1987), p. 147 and Table VII.

[48]*Ibid.*, p. 150 and Table VIII.

A significant aspect which has relevance for the postmaterialistic impact on support for the Community and unification is "cognitive mobilization." It suggests that "those with higher status occupations and incomes tend to be better educated, better informed about politics, and more active politically than the rest of their compatriots." People with these attributes are likely to feel relatively comfortable with large scale institutions such as are found in the EC and in discussions of politics may attempt to persuade their discussion partners—friends, relatives, or co-workers—to adopt their views and attitudes with respect to the Community and unification. Those who frequently and vigorously make these attempts are considered to be high on cognitive mobilization and to have a more supportive attitude toward the European Community than those who lack the above attributes.[49] But, as recent opinion surveys indicate, this linkage between cognitive mobilization and supportive Community attitudes seems to have weakened during the 1980s, although cognitive mobilization continued to remain conducive to attitudes supportive of the EC.[50]

Finally, when analyzing support for the Community and unification among the publics of the EC member states, a distinction is useful between "utilitarian" and "affective" support. Utilitarian support refers to "calculated appraisal of the immediate costs and benefits of membership in the Community," while affective or "diffuse" support relates to general efforts toward uniting Europe. The latter is not contingent on immediate payoffs, but economic benefits in earlier years are likely to strengthen affective support which requires an emotional base and time to grow.[51] Hence, it is not surprising that 1982–85 surveys show a lag of affective support among some of the newer member states compared with the original Six; moreover, respondents in all of the newer member states offered substantially less utilitarian support than was found among the original publics.[52]

In 1989, affective support for unification throughout the EC was 80 percent, with even the British sample showing 70 percent support and the lowest figure being Denmark, at 56 percent. As for utilitarian support, the responses in the survey during the first part of the 1980s were much more differentiated with

---

[49]*Ibid.*, p. 147.

[50]*Ibid.* and Table VI. It also seems that the Community has gained greater support among the less educated and politicized.

[51]*Ibid.*, p. 141 and Table I.

[52]Different survey organizations may come up with differing results. In more recent surveys in West Germany (1989), 24 percent of the respondents saw "advantages" in EC membership, 31 percent "disadvantages," and 44 percent thought they balanced each other out (*Frankfurter Allgemeine Zeitung*, June 8, 1989).

the support lowest in Great Britain (35 percent) and Denmark (37 percent). While the degree of utilitarian support remains a significant aspect of value change, the extent of affective support for European unification may well be deepened by a decline in feelings of nationalism as evidenced by the 1981–82 World Values survey plus relevant Eurobarometer surveys.[53] Considering what has been happening since 1991 in the former Soviet Union, further movement away from national pride in Western Europe may have been expedited and the trend to postmaterialism may have been enhanced.

## V. CONCLUSIONS

The basically sociological theories presented here all have the flavor of reasonableness with respect to explaining the possibility of political integration in the European Community. An increase of joint economic rewards and a reduction of economic deprivations produced by the forthcoming effects by "1992" may entail a stronger support and enthusiasm for political integration. Expanding transactions among the member states of various types, not only trade, but those resulting in the intensification of consumer values could also enhance the potential for European unification. Inglchart's concepts of post-materialism, if the predicted political perceptions and political circumstances are borne out as applicable for the present and early future, could provide an essential impetus for integration's forward movement. An underlying political culture could develop that would strengthen this movement.

But there are also powerful forces whose utilitarian interests and concerns may undermine the march toward unification and which are likely to seek, perhaps successfully, to retain the status quo. One such force emanates from domestic politics in all member states, maybe more in some than others, because holders of political power on national, subnational, and local levels do not want to lose or see reduced their exercise of power and their privileges as the Community institutions may gain power and influence. Another anti-integration force stems from the national and subnational bureaucracies who have similar apprehensions as the politicians of the member states and who also are likely to be jealous of their Eurocratic colleagues because the latters' involvements and privileges are higher than their own, and their taxes are lower. These are issues that need substantial future research which should offer important insights into the future of the Community.

---

[53]R. INGLEHART and K. REIF, Analyzing Trends in West European Opinion: The Role of the Eurobarometer Surveys, in K. REIF and R. INGLEHART (eds.), *Eurobarometer*, London, 1991, pp. 1–26, Table 1.4. See also Table 1.5.

## I. INTRODUCTION

Economic integration is in fashion again as an academic subject after a lapse of almost two decades. This has certainly something to do with the renewal of the process since 1985 in the most successful integration scheme of our century, namely the European Community. Not only is the internal market being completed, but the project of creating a monetary union before the end of this decade does not seem farfetched. This article will try to explain how the thinking of economists has been evolving on this fascinating subject over the last 40 years. In fact, until the mid-1970s theoreticians had a quite skeptical opinion about the economic value of customs union formation. It was considered to be a second best policy among others. With the development of the theory of intra-industry trade in the mid-1970s, new light was shed on the usefulness of regional trade liberalization. Economies of scale and the size of the market were entered into the new models in one way or another. Even more optimism about the role of economic integration was brought in when economists tried to investigate the effects of eliminating non-tariff barriers (NTBs) instead of customs duties. This was a reflection of the tremendous success not only of the EC and EFTA but also of GATT in reducing over the years the levels of tariff protection world-wide. All this leaves the reader of the relevant literature with the feeling that the economic profession recognizes now, maybe with a delay of several decades over their political science colleagues, that discriminatory trading arrangements tend to be welfare-increasing provided they are regionally based and fairly open to new membership.

## II. THE STATE OF THE THEORY IN THE MID-1960s

Until Jacob Viner published his pioneering work in 1950,[1] economic integration did not become a separate subject in economic theory. Between its

---

*I would like to thank Jacques Pelkmans for invaluable comments on a previous draft of this chapter. This article first appeared in Revue d'ntegration européenne/Journal of European Integration, vol. XV, no. 1 (Fall, 1991), pp. 5–23.

[1]J. VINER, *The Customs Union Issue*, New York, 1950. For a history of thought in economic integration, see F. MACHLUP, *A History of Thought on Economic Integration*, London, 1977.

A. **Developments in the Vinerian Analysis**

The concepts suggested more than 40 years ago by Viner (trade creation and diversion) have been accepted by every scholar of international trade theory, and as a matter of fact by most political economists, although they have had a lesser impact on the way practical policy-makers think. That a customs union can lead to a substitution of domestic high-cost sources by low-cost imports from associated countries does not seem to surprise anybody. What is already less obvious is that in many other cases the regional liberalization of trade can lead to a substitution of low-cost imports (which originated traditionally in non-member countries) by imports originating in one preferred member country. Viner thus stressed the discriminatory aspects of regional trade liberalization, showing by the same token that preferential concessions made on customs duties would impose real costs on the donors. This point is stressed here because it had been admitted earlier and rather frequently that such an agreement could affect negatively those excluded from it. What Viner said is that the welfare cost

---

[2]M. KRAUSS, Recent Developments in Customs Union Theory: An Interpretive Survey, *Journal of Economic Literature*, vol. 10 (1972), pp. 413–436.

[3]J. VINER, *op. cit.*

[4]J. MEADE, *The Theory of Customs Unions*, Amsterdam, 1955; and R. LIPSEY, The Theory of Customs Unions: Trade Diversion and Welfare, *Economica*, vol. 24 (1957), pp. 40–46.

[5]H. JOHNSON, An Economic Theory of Protection, Tariff Bargaining and the Formation of Customs Unions, *Journal of Political Economy*, vol. 73 (1965), vol. 72, pp. 256–283; and H. JOHNSON, Optimal Trade Intervention in the Presence of Domestic Distortions, in B. BALDWIN *et al.* (eds.), *Trade, Growth and the Balance of Payments*, Chicago, 1965, pp. 3–34.

[6]C. COOPER and B. MASSELL, A New Look at Customs Unions Theory, *Economic Journal*, vol. 75 (1965), pp. 742–747.

derived from trade diversion is borne by the consumers of the member countries, not by the exporters of third countries.[7]

Viner's analysis was clear-cut. However, his assumptions were very simplistic (something which, as we will see, did not detract from the general validity of his conclusion). In spite of this, it is convenient to mention at least two key assumptions.

First, production costs of future partner countries were supposed to be constant, whatever the amount produced. Therefore, the "rent" or "excess profit" element on the producer's side did not appear in the analysis. When using supply curves which reflect increasing costs, this missing feature must be reintroduced. It appears now that the constant cost assumption adopted by Viner was quite providential, since the level of both the non-discriminatory customs duty and the preferential customs duty decide in that case which country is going to be the *sole* supplier of the importing country. When there is trade creation, the protected domestic producer is the only supplier before the agreement while the producer of the associated country will be the one afterwards. If there is trade diversion, exports originating in non-member countries are entirely replaced. But if there are variable costs, a much more likely occurrence, trade patterns change less dramatically. According to Michaely,[8] there is nothing in Viner's writings which indicates that he assumed constant costs. It appears indeed that Viner stated sometimes that his theory applied in practice to the constant cost case but that is could be extended *telle quelle* to a model assuming variable costs. Here Viner erred because in that case any discriminatory trade liberalization contains simultaneously elements of trade creation and diversion, since the promotion of production in the preferred country is obtained at the expense *both* of the preference-giving country and of the non-member country. This result contrasts clearly with Viner's who had said very explicitly that in any given situation there would be *either* trade creation *or* diversion, but not both at the same time.

Second, Viner's analysis focussed on resource allocation changes and on production efficiency. However, it did not say anything on the reaction of the consumer's demand when domestic prices decrease as a result of customs union formation. Basic economics tells us that any price reduction has a positive impact on welfare, known as the "consumer's surplus." The latter is more or less important depending on the demand's price-elasticity. Focussing on this secondary positive effect, Lipsey[9] and others asserted that a trade-diverting

[7]Unfortunately, minimizing trade diversion is rarely in the agenda of the policy-maker. When it is, the latter has fiscal considerations in mind rather than the interest of consumers.

[8]M. MICHAELY, The Assumptions of Jacob Viner's Theory of Customs Unions, *Journal of International Economics*, vol. 6 (1976), pp. 75–93.

[9]R. LIPSEY, *loc. cit.*

customs union could be beneficial for its members, something contradicting openly Viner's conclusions. It is obvious that the consumer surplus effect can compensate in excess the negative trade diversion effect on the production side, provided the decrease in local prices is sufficiently large. As a result of Lipsey's attack on Viner, a discussion developed around the question of what Viner had or had not said, which is something to be left to historians of economic thought.[10] Krauss[11] ended the debate by insisting rightly that what is important is not to put tags on customs unions according to their positive or negative production effects, because the net effect on welfare depends as well on the effect on consumption.

## B. Why Are Customs Unions Created at All?

In the mid-1960s there appeared two professional articles[12] which had tremendous influence subsequently and which approach integration issues from a totally new viewpoint. Both state that Viner's theory is a sheer extension of free trade theory, since the trade creation effect is not more than what the integrative process contributes in terms of dismantling of protection in future partner countries and therefore can only be considered a step in the right direction. On the other hand, the trade diversion effect is damaging because it results in the introduction of new obstacles to the entry in the union of goods which were the cheapest in the world. Of course, the corollary of all this was quite logically that prospective partners could obtain the positive effects deriving from customs union formation by dismantling tariffs unilaterally without discriminating among foreign suppliers. In other words, according to Johnson and Cooper and Massell, trade integration must be understood as a special mechanism of

---

[10]J. MEADE (*op. cit.*) explained early on that ignoring effects on demand could be accepted only if explicitly assuming zero demand elasticities in the model. But he did not accuse Viner of making this assumption. Later on, Lipsey, Corden and Krauss assumed that in Viner's model goods must have been consumed in fixed proportions without any relation with changing relative prices. The debate was extended by J. BHAGWATI, Trade-Diverting Customs Unions and Welfare Improvement: A Clarification, *The Economic Journal*, vol. 81 (1971), pp. 580–587, vol. 81; and by A. KIRMAN, Trade-Diverting Customs Unions and Welfare Improvement: A Comment, *Economic Journal*, vol. 83 (1973), pp. 890–894. M. MICHAELY (*op. cit.*) went back to the original texts and concluded that Viner did not say any of the things that Lipsey attributed to him. Apparently Viner dwelled indirectly with the consumption effect, which he considered of less importance in practice and about which, he said, an economist could not make a normative statement.

[11]M. KRAUSS, *loc cit.*

[12]H. JOHNSON, *loc. cit.*, and C. COOPER and B. MASSELL, *loc. cit.*

protection which must be compared to other alternative instruments and not as a means for liberalizing trade. This viewpoint was rather original in that, around the same period, final shape was being given to a theory which gave a logical justification to government intervention in the presence of market failures.[13] The theory argues that although tariff protection can help in correcting market distortions, it will, in turn, create damaging secondary effects. In this way, non-discriminatory tariff protection is integrated among a range of policy instruments in the hands of governments to correct distortions. Corden went the farthest in this direction.[14] He ranked hierarchically all the available instruments according to the number of secondary distortions that the former introduce when they are used. And of course, depending on the initial distortion, tariff protection can be either the first best instrument, or the second, the third and so on.

Obviously the same type of analysis can be applied to the use of discriminatory tariffs. For instance, Johnson and Cooper and Massell assume that in many developing countries there is a collective preference for industrialization which is not properly taken into account by the market economy. In other words, it is thought that industrial activity must be promoted, even if the law of one price says otherwise, because such activity generates external economies, which are not visible. An old fashioned way of promotion is to introduce a prohibitive tariff on competing industrial imports. But the amount of new local production may still be insufficient, particularly if the local market is small. A production subsidy could be added. Johnson asks if one could not add markets of other countries to serve such a policy so that the promotion of local industry does not become too expensive. The idea here is that foreign markets will become "captive" once included in the preferential area. Any preferential tariff reduction allows the preferred country to capture a market share at the expense of non-members. In the presence of market failures of the kind assumed by Johnson, any trade diversion effect appears as beneficial and any tariff concession leading to a reduction of import substitution as welfare-decreasing. Exchanging preferential tariff concessions allows the two partners to share industrial markets at minimum cost in terms of menace to local producers.

In fact, all this literature on distortions shows that in the presence of market failures, the discriminatory intervention of government in trade matters may be justified, but it shows as well that in general there are better instruments to achieve the same results. This is always the case if distortions are of domestic origin; the analysis shows moreover that, if used at all, the tools used to discriminate geographically should be set at some optimal level so as to compensate exactly the initial distortion. In order to justify the creation of preferential trading arrangements one must assume that there are economic or

---

[13]The most relevant article is J. BHAGWATI, *loc. cit.*

[14]M. CORDEN, Economies of Scale and Customs Union Theory, *Journal of Political Economy*, vol. 80 (1972), pp. 465–475.

political constraints preventing the use of better instruments set at the right level (such as an optimal subsidy or an optimal tariff).

For instance, if the collective preference is for industrialization, a customs union is not the first best instrument to address it. Even if the public good ("the collective preference") in country A is for "more autonomy or self-sufficiency," a non-discriminatory restriction to trade is the first best instrument. Only if there is such an objective as "the need to trade with a given country (B) rather than with another (C) for political motives" or the "need to be independent from C" (e.g., the US), the first best policy is a customs union agreement between A and B.[15]

But when one makes these assumptions the danger is that any objective that a government may have may be called a collective preference, even if blurred or badly defined, and can lead to tremendous abuse. Even if the public good is really socially representative, it could be that it is irrational or that it collides head-on with the basic assumption in economics whereby "more is better than less," since then there is no sense whatsoever to engage in economic calculus.

In spite of this author's reservations, the merit of all this research was that it tried to explain why customs unions are established at all. Neoclassical trade theory had considered customs unions a second best from an economic viewpoint. The discovery that creating customs unions for economic reasons was rational was important in itself, since before it, most economists believed that the real reasons for establishing unions were political, sentimental or cultural. This is what neoclassical economists were saying until Johnson contradicted head-on the philosophy of those, like J. Monnet, creating the European Community, the only really successful integration scheme. The latter believed that the net economic benefits of regional cooperation would be so large that political and cultural obstacles would melt down with time, not the other way round!

## III. DEVELOPMENTS OF THE THEORY SINCE THE MID-1960s

Since 1965, research has been shifting in four different directions:

- research on the impact of integration agreements on the terms of trade;
- theoretical analysis of how scale economies and imperfect competition affect the basic model;
- extension of customs union theory to other forms of integration;
- extension of the theory in the presence of uncertainty and of non-tariff barriers (NTBs).

---

[15] A. EL AGRAA and A. JONES, *Theory of Customs Unions*, London, 1981.

## A. The Impact of Integration Agreements on the Terms of Trade

In the last two decades, theory has been looking at the experience of the European Community and has tried to understand why it was created at all. Very soon it appeared to several theoreticians that probably the error from Meade on had been to assume infinite supply elasticities of all foreign suppliers, thus ignoring terms of trade effects and ultimately making of unilateral dismantling the optimal policy. This is what had dominated trade theory through the 1960s and early 1970s. But the tendency to conclude integration agreements cannot be explained if one does not take into account the benefits of discrimination for the discriminators. This change of accent took place, not surprisingly, in the early 1970s at a moment trade relations between the US and the EC began to sour. This change has, then, to do with the redistribution of income among the three actors in any model of economic integration (the at least two members and the non-member(s)), i.e., it has to do with changes in the terms of trade between members and non-members.

Such effects had been examined early on by Mundell[16] and Vanek,[17] but much more thoroughly by Kemp,[18] Negishi[19] and Caves.[20] Pearce[21] stated clearly that the aim of a customs union is to redistribute world income in favour of the member countries through an improvement of the terms of trade with the rest of the world. This positive effect for the members must be placed against the neoclassical alternative of unilaterally dismantling tariffs on a non-discriminatory basis and which *caeteris paribus* leads to a deterioration of the terms of trade, not an improvement. In reality, says Pearce, creating a customs union for this purpose is akin to introducing an optimal trade restriction at the national level (i.e., optimal tariff theory). Customs union formation can be particularly advisable for small countries which cannot individually affect the

---

[16]R. MUNDELL, Tariff Preferences and the Terms of Trade, *Manchester School of Economic and Social Studies*, vol. 32 (1964), pp. 1–13.

[17]J. VANEK, *General Equilibrium of International Discrimination*, Cambridge, Mass., 1965.

[18]M. KEMP, *A Contribution to the General Equilibrium Theory of Preferential Trading*, Amsterdam, 1969.

[19]T. NEGISHI, Customs Unions and the Theory of the Second Best, *International Economic Review*, vol. 10 (1969), pp. 391–398.

[20]R. CAVES, The Economics of Reciprocity: Theory and Evidence on Bilateral Trading Arrangements, in W. SELLEKAERTS (ed.), *International Trade and Finance: Essays in Honour of Jan Tinbergen*, London, 1974, pp. 17–54.

[21]I. PEARCE, *International Trade*, vol. 1, London, 1970.

terms of trade. When joining a customs union, the country can do with its partners what it cannot do alone.

The contribution of the general equilibrium models of Vanek, Kemp, Negishi, and Caves was in focussing on the distribution of gains among member countries, and among them and non-members. The main conclusion was that the country which traded before the union mainly with its future partner was likely to gain from the integration, whereas partners with large trade stakes in the rest of the world would lose. All this would hold unless the latter were able to improve their terms of trade with the rest of the world through trade diversion in such a way as to compensate for the deadweight loss derived from being led to switch supply sources. But the improvement of the terms of trade depends on the relative size of the union in relation to third countries. Kemp, in a very influential article written with Wan,[22] extended his previous analysis by stating very simply that customs union formation was a positive contribution to world welfare (therefore contradicting Viner) inasmuch as it was also possible for the partner who gains to compensate fully the loser inside and the non-members outside, and still be better off. This could always be done, first, by a series of intra-union lump-sum transfers and, second, by picking the right Common External Tariff (CET) instead of assuming that the latter was equal either to the tariff prevailing before in the importing country or to an arithmetic average of the members' tariffs before the union was formed. Manipulating the CET allows the elimination of any trade diversion cost (and by the same token any terms of trade effect). Therefore, after the mid-1970s, theoretical optimism came back through the back door: customs unions were not irrational creatures after all, even if, as Berglas[23] showed later, in the absence of domestic distortions anything which the member countries could gain by preferential trading could be gained by unilaterally dismantling the tariff.[24]

All the attempts of the late 1970s and early 1980s to obtain more clear-cut conclusions, beyond what Berglas had proven, by trying to add more goods and more countries to the basic 2x2 neoclassical model failed.[25] On the

---

[22]M. KEMP and H. WAN, An Elementary Proposition Concerning the Formation of Customs Unions, *Journal of International Economics*, vol. 6 (1976), pp. 95–97.

[23]E. BERGLAS, Preferential Trading Theory: The n-Commodity Case, *Journal of Political Economy*, vol. 87 (1979), pp. 315–331; and E. BERGLAS, The Case for Unilateral Tariff Reductions: Foreign Tariffs Rediscovered, *The American Economic Review*, vol. 73 (1983), pp. 1141–1142.

[24]More recently, Nicolaides has been able to show that a free trade agreement (but not a customs union) may be superior even to unilateral tariff reductions; P. NICOLAIDES, A General Equilibrium Method for Evaluating Customs Unions, *Economia Internazionale*, vol. 41:3–4 (1988), pp. 216–224.

[25]R. RIEZMAN, A Theory of Customs Unions: The Three Country Two-Good Case, *Weltwirtschaftliches Archiv*, vol. 115 (1979), pp. 701–715; P.

contrary, all these "3x3" models only blurred further an already confusing analysis looking for reasons why countries engage in discriminatory trading arrangements. To cap it all, a rather sour note has been added more recently to the debate on the terms of trade. Krugman[26] has pointed to the obvious fact that the optimal Common External Tariff should be expected to be higher than the pre-union tariff rates of the member nations, given their increased market power derived from acting jointly. On the basis of Kemp and Wan's 1976 findings, the proof that customs unions were potentially good for the world relied on the fact that the latter could always prevent trade diversion. But Krugman expects customs unions always to provoke trade diversion as part and parcel of their *raison d'être*, leading in all likelihood to a reduction of non-members' welfare and, in some cases, of the world's welfare as a whole (see more on this below).

## IV. THEORETICAL ANALYSIS OF THE IMPACT OF SCALE ECONOMIES

The argument for creating economic unions to better exploit scale economies which cannot be reaped in small national markets relies on the basic idea that mass production reduces average costs per unit. However, this is a general argument for trade liberalization or for world-wide free trade. And all depends obviously on the type of product in question and the relative size of the national market when compared to the union's market. Corden[27] analyzed what the argument implies in practice and showed that apart from the usual trade creation and trade diversion effects, there are two supplementary effects to count on, one positive, one negative. The positive one is the cost reduction effect. The customs union leads to cost reductions also in the quantity locally supplied previously (under prohibitive protection) by the most efficient producer in the union. On top of this, it supplies the other members of the union, hence there is a trade creation effect. But Corden says that there could also be a trade suppression effect whenever all the partner countries were before the union importing all consumption from non-members (because there was no tariff or the latter was not high enough to be prohibitive). After the customs union is created, the least inefficient partner country may be able to begin producing simply because now it has all the union's markets at its disposal and this may

COLLIER, The Welfare Effects of Customs Unions: An Anatomy, *The Economic Journal*, vol. 89 (1979), pp. 84–95; J. MCMILLAN and E. MCCANN, Welfare Effects in Customs Unions, *The Economic Journal*, vol. 91 (1981), pp. 697–703; and P. LLOYD, 3x3 Theory of Customs Unions, *Journal of International Economics*, vol. 12 (1982), pp. 41–63.

[26]P. KRUGMAN, Increasing Returns and Economic Geography, *NBER Working Paper Series, No. 3245*, 1990.

[27]M. CORDEN, *loc. cit.*

be sufficient to have average unit costs in the area become smaller than the price-cum-common external tariff set by the union. Other member countries suffer from trade diversion in favor of the exporting country.

The scale economies argument has been combined in the 1970s with the fast-growing theory of intra-industry trade, developed initially by Grubel and Lloyd,[28] which opposes it to the Hecksher-Ohlin type of theories of inter-industry trade.[29] Observed intra-EC two-way trade in differentiated products and the related intra-industry specialization, they say, is probably due to a concentration of local EC producers in particular production lines and models once they are assured that they will enjoy a quasi-monopoly in the whole EC market for the particular brand they produce.[30] Economists speak of monopolistic competition. Not surprisingly, in the 1980s the scale economies argument has been progressively linked to new models of international trade under imperfect competition, drawing abundantly from industrial economics.[31]

The interesting question is to know if customs union creation is a substitute or a complement to competition policy. It used to be thought that trade liberalization could replace competition policy insofar as local monopolies would be kept in check by international competition. The argument is back in fashion in connection with the expected benefits of completing the EC's internal market.[32] But if the starting assumption is that there were unexploited economies of scale before (regional) trade liberalization, the latter will increase concentration and firm scale, and ultimately justify mass production which is incompatible with perfect competition. After a quasi-monopoly in differentiated products is established in every partner country, the latter may be tempted to jack up prices to whatever the traffic can bear. Smith and Venables seem to think

---

[28]H. GRUBEL and P. LLOYD, *Intra-Industry Trade*, London, 1975.

[29]Inter-industry specialization is based on comparative advantage which is, in turn, explained by different relative factor endowments or by the existence of different technologies in the various trading countries.

[30]It is actually not very important in which brand each of the producers specializes, provided they specialize! In other words, trade is not based on comparative advantage and the direction of trade is indeterminate.

[31]P. KRUGMAN (ed.), *Strategic Trade Policy and the New International Economics*, Cambridge, Mass., 1986; W. ETHIER and H. HORN, A New Look at Economic Integration, in H. KIERZKOWSKY (ed.), *Monopolistic Competition and International Trade*, Oxford, 1984, pp. 207–229; E. HELPMAN and P. KRUGMAN, *Market Structure and Foreign Trade: Increasing Returns, Imperfect Competition and the International Economy*, Cambridge, Mass., 1985; and A. SMITH and A. VENABLES, Completing the Internal Market in the EC: Some Industry Simulations, *European Economic Review*, vol. 32, no. 7 (1988), pp. 1501–1525.

[32]A. SMITH and A. VENABLES, *loc. cit.*

that products exchanged across borders are sufficiently similar for this not to happen. Interestingly, they show that the gains of removing intra-union trade barriers in such a setting are generally modest. What in their view makes a big difference is the fact that nationally based monopolistic firms prevailing before the union is created can no longer apply a price-discriminating strategy; market segmentation is not feasible. Domestic markets are no longer captive. On the other hand, local firms can no longer dump goods across borders at prices below costs, something feasible whenever they can cover losses by selling domestically at monopolistic prices. The forced reduction of domestic prices and the increase in intra-union export prices leads to less, rather than more, intra-union trade.[33] Nonetheless, there is still a need for competition policies to follow in case the final or intermediary consumer perceives the products exchanged as rather different. Competition policies must complement economic integration to prevent monopoly power resurfacing at the union level.[34] As Jacquemin and Sapir[35] argue, competition policy is one of the most important guarantees for the internal and external liberalization of a common market. The advantage of competition policy over trade policy is that it is rule-based. There is almost no role left for discretion. But Jacquemin and Sapir go one step further when they say that, in the future, domestic competition policy may not be enough in order to reap the benefits of integration. Only the establishment of worldwide competition rules will suffice.

On the other hand, the new theoretical developments point in a different direction as far as trade policy is concerned. In the world of increasing returns, "first mover advantages" are critical. The temptation for a government is then to intervene to promote production in the desired direction and preempt the entry of competing countries to the fray. This is what economists call "strategic trade policy."[36] However, when sovereign countries decide to integrate they are, in fact, stating that they foreclose autonomous intervention, i.e., that they renounce the implementation of an individual trade policy. They prefer (or accept) that intervention be done at the level of the union. Is there a reason to believe that "strategic trade policy" is better conducted at the union's level than at the national level? The answer is an unqualified yes, since the internal market is larger. However, it is also much more difficult to reach a consensus among

---

[33]A. VENABLES, The Economic Integration of Oligopolistic Markets, *European Economic Review*, vol. 34, no. 4 (1990), pp. 753–773; and P. KRUGMAN, Increasing Returns, Monopolistic Competition and International Trade, *op. cit.*

[34]R.C. HINE, *The Political Economy of European Trade*, New York, 1985.

[35]A. JACQUEMIN and A. SAPIR, Europe Post-1992: Internal and External Liberalization, *American Economic Review*, vol. 81, no. 2 (1991), pp. 166–170.

[36]P. KRUGMAN, Increasing Returns and Economic Geography, *NBER Working Paper, No. 3245*, 1990.

member countries on what product to promote since such a decision will favour one member over the other. Therefore, compared to the world of constant returns to scale, in the presence of economies of scale, economic integration may lead not only to more conflictive relations between members and non-members (which could end in trade wars), but also to more friction among member countries, unless the latter play a cooperative game both among themselves or with other strategic actors.

## V. EXTENSION OF THE THEORY OF CUSTOMS UNIONS TO OTHER FORMS OF INTEGRATION

Until the late 1960s, it was fashionable, following Viner, to analyze the special case of customs unions but add a few sentences stating that conclusions could be extended *telles quelles* to free trade areas, partial preferential agreements or common markets. Since then a series of studies have appeared which show clearly the originality of each of these other integration forms.[37] In the case of free trade areas (FTAs), Shibata showed that there is a shifting effect, i.e., an indirect or of trade deflection which origin rules cannot pre-empt. Without the latter, an FTA would become a customs union which adopts a CET equal to that of the country with high tariffs would lose all revenue and the national tariff would become obsolete. However, even with rules of origin the tariff *is partially obsolete*. The low-tariff country can satisfy all local demand after the FTA is formed with imports from non-members and gear import-competing production to serve the high-tariff country market. Net trade diversion is less than the amount previously imported from non-members in the high-tariff country since the low-tariff country imports more from non-members. Furthermore, net trade diversion can be negative, i.e., there may be external trade creation. Another original feature of FTAs is that, generally speaking, there is not a single price in the area (as in customs unions). Of course shifting effects are more likely the closer member countries are geographically. This may explain why there are not many FTAs among neighbours: high tariff countries are naturally hostile to trade deflection and shifting effects. Theoreticians tend to think that FTAs are a more liberal form of integration than tariff-averaging customs unions and probably more welfare-increasing. The low tariff country is not compelled to raise its tariff in the FTA case and can thus preempt trade destruction, while domestic prices in the high tariff country may go down

---

[37]H. SHIBATA, A Theory of Free Trade Areas, in P. ROBSON (ed.), *International Economic Integration*, Harmondsworth, 1971; V. CURZON, *The Essentials of Economic Integration*, London, 1974; A. TOVIAS, *Tariff Preferences in Mediterranean Diplomacy*, London, 1977; P. WONNACOTT and M. LUTZ, Is There a Case for Free Trade Areas? in J. SCHOTT (ed.), *Free Trade Areas and US Trade Policy*. Washington, DC, 1989; and I. WOOTON, Preferential Trading Agreements: An Investigation, *Journal of International Economics*, vol. 21 (1986), pp. 81–97. P. ROBSON, *The Economics of International Integration*, London, 3rd edition.

(provided the low tariff country can entirely replace nonmembers' imports) as in the case of a tariff-averaging customs union. Of course, terms of trade effects are also less likely.

Economists agree as well that customs unions are not superior to partial preferential trade arrangements, in spite of the doctrine of GATT. Moreover, in the latter case, customs revenue does not decrease in the same proportions as in customs unions or FTAs; it may even increase. This may be important for members unable to find alternative fiscal sources to fund their budgets. Insofar as the profession distrusts government intervention in foreign trade because it is always protectionistic, it favours the customs union formula because of its "all-or-nothing" character. Members cannot design preferential concessions so as to maximize trade diversion and minimize trade creation. The "all-or-nothing" and irreversible character of a customs union adds to the attractiveness of the formula over partial agreements in case increasing returns are widespread. In that respect, note that the reason why FTAs are sometimes preferred over customs unions is that the former allow for exceptions while still being compatible with GATT rules, unlike preferential trade agreements (e.g., agriculture is excluded in EFTA).

The theory of common markets is less developed. In fact, factor market integration has, with few exceptions,[38] hardly been addressed.[39] The latter examines whether member countries of a customs union would gain from moving to a common market and proves that this depends on the level chosen for the CET. If the latter is adjusted at appropriate levels, building a common market is welfare-increasing.

## VI. EXTENSION OF THE THEORY IN THE PRESENCE OF UNCERTAINTY AND OF NTBs

A recent argument in favour of customs unions is that they are a kind of insurance policy against world price uncertainty for small countries which even together cannot influence world prices.[40] The paradox is that once uncertainty disappears there is an incentive to opt out, although there is then a cost to the reputation of members which do not honour their signatures.

---

[38]B. BALDWIN, Factor Market Barriers Are Trade Barriers, *European Economic Review*, vol. 34 (June 1990), No. 4; and I. WOOTON, Towards a Common Market: Factor Mobility in a Customs Union, *Journal of International Economics*, vol. 21 (1986), pp. 81–97.

[39]Although, as Pelkmans says, capital market integration has been analyzed in the context of "open macroeconomics." J. PELKMANS, EC-1992 as a Challenge to Economic Analysis, *CEPS Working Document No. 53*, 1990.

[40]T. FRIES, Uncertainty as a Possible Rationale for Customs Unions, *Journal of International Economics*, vol. 17, nos. 3–4 (1984), pp. 347–357.

Turning now to the NTBs, the distinction between trade creation and diversion remains critical for evaluating integration schemes,[41] even though the case against trade diversion associations has been muddled by the shift to this kind of barriers as a method of protection. For instance, a selective relaxation of QRs in favour of member countries without a simultaneous tightening of QRs applied on nonmembers does provoke trade diversion but does not impose costs on importing countries[42] and does not come either at the expense of the outside world.[43] The idea that trade diversion is undesirable for member countries is generally valid only when tariffs are the means of protection. Pelkmans and Winters[44] show that when barriers which are removed among members are not revenue-generating (as tariffs are) but cost-increasing (such as differing testing and certification requirements or cumbersome customs procedures), the diversion of trade in favour of union members is not welfare-reducing. However, in practice, what happens is that union members first create a customs union and only then decide to eliminate cost-increasing NTBs among them. When they engage in this second step, trade diversion is welfare-reducing after all because revenue previously generated by the CET imposed on nonmembers' imports is lost.[45] The EC eradicated intra-EC quotas right from the start. Public purchase and sale monopolies in member states were also outlawed by the Treaty of Rome. But other NTBs, such as technical barriers, have not been removed until recently, so that Sapir's argument applies to the EC as well.

The elimination of different NTBs in the integration area has been explicitly treated only recently, as a reaction to plans by the EC to complete its internal market by January 1, 1993. Winters,[46] for example, shows that replacing QRs on the transhipment of third country goods among members of a union (which had been imposed in the first place to prevent trade deflection) is welfare-increasing.[47] However, in practice, it is likely that individual member

---

[41]P. WONNACOTT and M. LUTZ, *loc. cit.*

[42]Although as indicated by J. PELKMANS and A. WINTERS, *Europe's Domestic Market*, London, 1988, it may reduce quota rents cashed by local importers.

[43]W. MOLLE, *The Economics of European Integration*, Aldershot, 1990.

[44]J. PELKMANS and A. WINTERS, *op. cit.*

[45]A. SAPIR, Does 1992 Come Before or After 1990?, in R. JONES and A. KRUEGER (eds.), *The Political Economy of International Trade*, Oxford, 1989, pp. 197–222.

[46]A. WINTERS, Completing the European Internal Market, *European Economic Review*, vol. 32 (1988), pp. 1477–1499.

[47]This conclusion is not surprising. It is quite equivalent to abolishing origin rules in the case of an FTA agreement.

states will then request from the center the imposition of a common quota equal to or less than the sum of member states' quotas so as to leave the situation as it was in the most restrictive countries.

Switching now to another important NTB, namely, discriminatory government procurement, Tovias[48] shows that its abolition by member countries and further replacement by preferential government procurement at the union level can lead to proportionately larger trade diversion or suppression than in the case of customs union formation. First of all, discriminatory procurement as a disguised subsidy to the local champion is not a cost-increasing distortion to trade, but rather a quasi-fiscal measure. As such, the surprising and very optimistic assessment of Pelkmans and Winters regarding other NTBs does not apply. Second, there is a negative consumption component to trade diversion which is absent in the case of customs unions. This is due to the fact that national governments or public agencies were free to buy equipment in world markets beyond a limited protected amount which had to be bought at home. After integration of public purchasing policies, it is most likely that all imports have to be bought from area suppliers at higher prices, therefore diminishing quantities bought.

I will not refer here to the analysis of the effects of eliminating in the area of integration NTBs on trade in services, because of lack of substantial work on the subject and of space limitations.[49]

## VII. WHERE DO WE STAND AT PRESENT?

In the 1980s a new consensus seemed to prevail whereby discriminatory trading arrangements are fully justified if they are regionally based and if members acting together can influence the terms of trade with the rest of the world, but not otherwise. Three principal theoretical contributions make the point on regional arrangements. Wonnacott and Wonnacott[50] show that whenever prospective partners have difficulties of access to third countries due to the existence of artificial barriers imposed by nonmembers or natural barriers separating members from nonmembers (something ignored in previous analysis),

---

[48]A. TOVIAS, The Impact of Liberalizing Government Procurement Policies of Individual EC Countries on Trade with Non-members, *Weltwirtschaftliches Archiv*, vol. 126, no. 4 (December 1990), pp. 722–736.

[49]See J. PELKMANS, EC–1992 as a Challenge to Economic Analysis, *loc. cit.*, for some further exploration of the subject. Pelkmans stresses the inspiration function of the so-called Cecchini Report, an empirical study commissioned by the EC on the probable impact of completing the Community's internal market.

[50]P. WONNACOTT and R. WONNACOTT, Is Unilateral Tariff Reduction Preferable to a Customs Union? The Curious Case of the Missing Foreign Tariffs, *The American Economic Review*, vol. 71 (1981), pp. 704–714.

unilateral tariff reduction by the country wishing to gain access to the prospective partner's market is not better than creating a customs union which reorients trade in favour of intra-regional trade. This trade diversion is not welfare-reducing but rather the contrary, because reorientation saves on transport costs. Krugman[51] has proven explicitly that the likelihood of a preferential trading agreement being welfare-increasing rises with the inherent regionalism of the members wishing to join. Countries of the same region were, before the union, probably doing a large part of their trade with neighbours anyway; therefore, trade diversion of the Viner kind will be small. Balassa and Bauwens[52] show that the existence of common borders and small distance is positively related to intra-industry trade. The former not only minimize transportation costs, but even more important, information costs, two key factors entering production functions of differentiated products. In short, common borders and short distances favour, in turn, intra-industry specialization and a better exploitation of national and international scale economies.

Economists have today also a clearer idea of why all this confusion about the worthiness of customs union creation developed. Most models of the 1960s and 1970s assumed implicitly that the integration scheme was being formed between a small country and a large country (or a group of countries) which were not neighbours, while the rest of the world was huge and would not notice what was going on. In that context, it can clearly be shown[53] that the small partner invariably gains, the large country invariably loses and non-members are indifferent. This model fits, to mention just three examples, what happened when the United Kingdom signed the EFTA agreement with six highly dispersed small European countries; when Portugal entered the EC; and when Israel signed a free trade agreement with the US. Curiously, with few exceptions,[54] no one seemed to be interested by the small country partner.

---

[51]P. KRUGMAN, *Increasing Returns and Economic Geography, op. cit.*

[52]B. BALASSA and L. BAUWENS, The Determinants of Intra-European Trade in Manufactured Goods, *European Economic Review*, no. 32 (1988), pp. 1421–1437.

[53]A. TOVIAS, Differential Country Size as an Incentive to the Proliferation of Trading Blocs, *Journal of Common Market Studies*, vol. 16, no. 3 (1978), pp. 246–266.

[54]See A. TOVIAS, *Tariff Preferences in Mediterranean Diplomacy, op. cit.*, and R. POMFRET and B. TOREN, *Israel and the European Common Market*, Tübingen, 1980. Viner paid little attention to the preference recipient country, probably because it could not improve benefits by expanding exports, since constant costs were assumed. Paradoxically, it was A. Smith who emphasized the gain to the preference recipient country, a point also largely forgotten in the 1960s by those proposing unilateral concessions by importing countries *in lieu* of creating a customs union which, as Smith sensed, helps as well to promote exports: A. SMITH, *An Inquiry Into the Nature and Causes of the Wealth of Nations*, New York, 1937.

Most theoreticians were questioning the economic rationale for entering such agreements of economies like the UK, the EC or the US in the examples just mentioned. Economists were right in thinking that the three had "only" political reasons in mind ("counter the creation of the EC," "create spheres of influence," "reinforce democracy"), knowing well in advance that there was a cost to all this in terms of trade diversion, with no improvement of the terms of trade with nonmembers to compensate for.

But clearly not all customs unions are signed on a nonregional basis by members of radically different economic sizes and not all unions created are "small" in world terms. If sizes are similar, reciprocity embodied in integration agreements insure that every member gains as an exporter. As an importer, it may sometimes lose (not always as in the large/small country model), but sometimes gain (because domestic prices drop after all imports have been diverted to the partner which, as assumed, is not so small and can service all the local market). This may have happened with the initial association of the four equally sized customs territories that were France, Italy, the Federal Republic of Germany and the Benelux in the formation of the EEC. Further, they constituted a "natural trading block" in Western Europe, from a geographical viewpoint, *à la* Krugman. Enlarging the EC from six to nine and then to twelve, always on a regional basis, added a supplementary attractiveness for the members in that they could begin to count more and more on improving their terms of trade with the rest of the world, since the EC evolved from a small "union" to a larger one.

Since the club was constituted by technologically advanced, developed countries, many of their production functions displayed increasing, not constant returns to scale. In such a setting, adding more members and enlarging the market increases the probability of having a firm in the club which is able to produce a good not previously available in the union (e.g., a supercomputer) at unit costs which are only marginally higher than those of the good previously imported from nonmembers. This minimizes Corden's trade suppression effect (which, in EC parlance, would come to the "cost of Fortress Europe" for the members). Moreover, as trade with the rest of the world shrinks it is likely that the cost of goods previously imported from nonmembers will rise since production is curtailed there.[55] In this kind of setting, the sooner non-member countries apply for membership, the better! However, the larger the share of member countries to nonmember countries, the less will the welfare of existing members increase. At some point, they may even lose. The reason is that "firms in countries already in the union gain liberalized access to one additional market (but) in which the price has fallen; the net effect of this on their profits is in general, ambiguous . . . ."[56] The issue of the increasing size of the union

---

[55]A. VENABLES, Customs Union and Tariff Reform Under Imperfect Competition, *European Economic Review*, vol. 31 (1987), pp. 103–110.

[56]A. VENABLES, *loc. cit.*, p. 109.

has been addressed more recently by Krugman.[57] He points to the simple fact that the larger the number of members the higher will be the optimal Common External Tariff.[58] This will increasingly close the union to the outside world, a clear indication that bilateralism in tariff matters tends to impair multilateralism unless major actors agree to play cooperatively. For senior members, the ongoing incorporation of new countries into the scheme does add fewer and fewer terms of trade gains in trade with the rest of the world and increases the burden of trade diversion to them. Of course, for latecomers, the larger the union the better, whereas for those staying outside exactly the contrary applies. Observe, however, that the idea is that for the world as a whole, welfare will be reduced with the increasing size of the union until a point is reached where, when there is a reduced number of unions, the situation is suddenly reversed[59] because the world approaches a state of universal tariff-free trade. What is said here is clearly relevant to the current discussions on whether the creation of tariff-free blocks in North America or in the Pacific Region would impair GATT or not. It is much less relevant, on the other hand, for analyzing the impact on multilateralism of an NTB-free block such as EC-92.

Note, as well, that there is clearly a link between what Tovias[60] or Pomfret and Toren[61] were saying about the distribution of gains among countries and the size of the union. The larger the union becomes, the larger is the disproportion of economic size between the union and the new members. It is not surprising that the latter play the role of the "small" country in the models of Tovias and Pomfret, while the union is in the position of their large country for which increasing welfare could not be the object of the agreement. What Krugman says is that the larger the tariff federation, the more irrational it is likely to be from an economic viewpoint unless it embraces practically the whole world.

This chapter has been dealing with what the theory of economic integration has achieved until now. There are still many omissions and much

---

[57] P. KRUGMAN, Is Bilateralism Bad?, *NBER Working Paper Series*, No. 2972, 1989.

[58] Observe that this argument applies only to revenue-generating barriers such as tariffs, but not to cost-increasing barriers such as technical regulations.

[59] Using a range of plausible values for some key variables, Krugman finds that the worst number of tariff unions is three.

[60] A. TOVIAS, Differential Country Size . . . , *loc. cit.*

[61] R. POMFRET and B. TOREN, *op. cit.*

remains to be done. The reader wishing to look ahead should consult Pelkmans[62] which maps for us the future agenda.

[62]J. PELKMANS, EC–1992 as a Challenge . . . , *loc. cit.*

# INTEGRATION THROUGH LAW: THE COURT OF JUSTICE AND THE ACHIEVEMENT OF THE SINGLE MARKET AND THE EUROPEAN UNION*

Alex EASSON
*Queen's University, Kingston*

## I. A COMMUNITY BASED UPON THE RULE OF LAW

The heads of state of the twelve member states of the European Community, "confirming their attachment to the principles of liberty, democracy and respect for human rights and fundamental freedoms and of the rule of law . . . HAVE DECIDED to establish a European Union . . . ." So reads the Preamble of the Maastricht Treaty,[1] confirming what the Court of Justice had emphasized some years previously in the *Les Verts* case, that the European Community "is a Community based on the rule of law, inasmuch as neither its Member States nor its institutions can avoid a review of the question whether the measures adopted by them are in conformity with the basic constitutional charter, the Treaty."[2]

Although the EEC Treaty itself nowhere employs the words "rule of law," the intention of the authors to endow the Community with its own legal system is clear from the creation of the Court of Justice, and from the jurisdiction conferred upon it, notably by Articles 169 and 170, Articles 173 and 175, and above all by Article 177. It is, admittedly, a somewhat peculiar legal system with, until recently, only one court, no bar, no public prosecutors (unless the Commission can be said to perform that role), no prisons, and very limited powers to impose sanctions. Nevertheless, it was certainly intended that at least some of the activities of the Community should be subject to judicial

---

*This essay is a substantially revised version of an article that appeared under the title, "Legal Approaches to European Integration: The Role of the Court and Legislator in the Completion of the European Common Market," in *Revue d'Intégration européenne/Journal of European Integration*, vol. XII, nos. 2–3 (1989), pp. 101–119.

[1]*Treaty on European Union*, Maastricht, December 11, 1991, Agence Europe, doc. no. 1759/60, February 7, 1992.

[2]Case 294/83, *Partie Ecologiste "Les Verts" v. European Parliament* [1986], E.C.R. 1339, p. 1365.

supervision. However, few could have predicted, in 1957, the extent to which the rule of law would prevail over the acts of the Community's institutions and of the member states, and the crucial role that the Court would play in the process of integration. Of all the Community's institutions, it is the Court of Justice that has been the most successful in promoting the objectives of the Treaty,[3] so that it can truly be said that, from a legal perspective—as well as from an economic and political point of view—the European Community would have been quite different had the Court of Justice not developed the key concepts of the direct effect and supremacy of Community law.[4] It is this process of "constitutionalization" of the Treaty, by the Court acting in its role of guardian of the Treaty, that has made the law such an effective tool in promoting integration. And this is complemented by the way in which the Court, acting as the authoritative interpreter of the Treaty, has defined the scope of the rights and obligations that flow from the Treaty.

## II. THE CONSTITUTIONALIZATION OF THE EEC TREATY

For a lawyer, and perhaps also for a political scientist, the most striking feature of the Community, and that which distinguishes it most clearly from other international groups or organizations of states, is the essentially federal nature of its legal system. What was in its initial conception a multipartite treaty has been transformed into a constitutional document[5] and the Court of Justice has evolved into a constitutional court.[6] That this is so is almost entirely the doing of the Court itself, for the "constitutionalization" of

---

[3]See, generally, M. CAPPELLETTI, M. SECCOMBE and J. WEILER (eds.), *Integration through Law*, Florence, 1986, and especially the contributions of the editors (Book 1, p. 51), of F. JACOBS and K. KARST (Book 1, p. 200), and of M. CAPPELLETTI and D. GOLAY (Book 2, p. 308).

[4]C.-D. EHLERMANN, The Second Wilberforce Lecture, *Common Market Law Review*, 29 (1992), p. 215.

[5]The Court itself, in *Les Verts* (see note 2), refers to the Treaty as a "basic constitutional charter." See also E. STEIN, Lawyers, Judges and the Making of a Transnational Constitution, *American Journal of International Law*, 75 (1981), p. 1; G.F. MANCINI, The Making of a Constitution for Europe, *Common Market Law Review*, 26 (1989), p. 595; K. LENAERTS, Constitutionalism and the Many Faces of Federalism, *American Journal of Comparative Law*, 38 (1990), p. 205.

[6]It is clearly viewed as such by one former justice of the Court: U. EVERLING, The Court of Justice as a Decision-Making Authority, *Michigan Law Review*, 82 (1984), p. 1294. See also K. LENAERTS, Some Reflections on the Separation of Powers in the European Community, *Common Market Law Review*, 28 (1991), p. 32, and the works of Justices LENAERTS and MANCINI, cited in note 5 above.

the EEC Treaty rests principally upon the twin concepts which it has developed, those of the direct effect and the supremacy of Community law.[7]

## A. Direct Effect

The literature on the concept of direct effect is extensive[8] and it is not intended here to examine the jurisprudence in detail, but in order to demonstrate its fundamental importance in the system of Community law it is appropriate to trace briefly the evolution of the concept. To do so, one must return to the famous *Van Gend en Loos* case,[9] arguably the single most important judgment ever delivered by the Court and one of the turning points in the history of the Community.

The facts of the case are simple. The Dutch government had increased the customs duties on certain products, contrary to Article 12 of the EEC Treaty, which had imposed a standstill obligation on the member states. The question posed by a Dutch tax court to the Court of Justice, under the preliminary ruling procedure of Article 177, was whether Article 12 had direct application, in the sense that nationals of member states could claim individual rights based thereon. The Dutch government, which was supported by the governments of Belgium and Germany, accepted that the article imposed obligations on the national governments. Consequently, it submitted, failure to fulfill those obligations might lead to proceedings against the offending state by the Commission, but until such time as the state rectified its breach, the courts of that state would be obliged to apply the offending national law. The Court of Justice, however, rejected that view and ruled that the obligation which the Treaty clearly and unconditionally imposed upon the member states gave rise to corresponding rights enforceable by individual citizens. In effect, an individual could rely upon the Treaty against an attempt by national authorities to impose a charge which contravened the Treaty.

Now the Treaty itself nowhere states what is to be the effect of Community law within the member states. It can reasonably be assumed that its authors intended some effect, otherwise there would be little point in Article

---

[7]J. WEILER, Community, Member States and European Integration: Is the Law Relevant?, *Journal of Common Market Studies*, 21 (1982-83), p. 42. See also the observations of another justice of the Court, LORD MACKENZIE STUART, *The European Communities and the Rule of Law*, London, 1977, p. 16, and of the former head of the Commission's Service Juridique, C.-D. EHLERMANN, note 4 above.

[8]See especially G. BEBR, *Development of Judicial Control of the European Communities*, The Hague, 1981, Chap. 13; P. PESCATORE, The Doctrine of "Direct Effect": An Infant Disease of Community Law, *European Law Review*, 8 (1983), p. 155.

[9]Case 26/62, *Van Gend en Loos* [1963], E.C.R. 1.

177 allowing or requiring national courts to seek rulings as to its interpretation. Those effects, nonetheless, might have been intended to be quite limited: treaty provisions are applied to a greater or lesser extent in most countries, even if this extends no further than a rule of interpretation that ambiguities in domestic legislation are to be resolved in a manner which is consistent with the state's international obligations. The Court of Justice was thus faced with a clear choice, between a literal approach—that the provision, being addressed only to states, was binding only upon them—thus observing the principle that transfers of sovereignty are to be interpreted narrowly, and a goal-oriented approach, seeking by interpretation to further social, economic and political integration.[10] In choosing the latter, the reasoning of the Court showed that "the judges had *une certaine idée de l'Europe* of their own."[11]

The impact of *Van Gend en Loos* becomes obvious when one considers what the Community would have been like without the principle of direct effect. In similar circumstances, the importer might have complained to the Commission that customs duty was being improperly imposed, the Commission would have made representations to the offending government, leading eventually to an action under Article 169 if the state did not remedy the situation, the Court would have condemned the infraction and, in due course, which might well have been five or six years, the offending legislation would have been amended.

All this changes as a consequence of direct effect. Individuals have an immediate remedy, in their own national courts, against the defaulting state. Moreover there is the immense advantage, from the point of view of the public perception, that Community law is seen to come to the assistance of private individuals. As the Court itself observed in *Van Gend en Loos*,

> [t]he vigilance of individuals concerned to protect their rights amounts to an effective supervision in addition to the supervision entrusted by Articles 169 and 170 to the diligence of the Commission and of the member states.

Individuals are thus given an incentive to raise issues of Community law before their national courts, which in turn may request preliminary rulings from the Court of Justice under Article 177. This affords the Court further opportunity to interpret the Treaty and the secondary legislation of the institutions, thereby further defining and refining the concepts of Community law.[12]

---

[10]See H. RASMUSSEN, *On Law and Policy in the European Court of Justice*, Dordrecht, 1986, p. 12.

[11]P. PESCATORE, note 8 above, p. 157.

[12]By the end of 1987, the Court had delivered rulings in 1,317 cases under Article 177, and had decided 243 cases under the direct procedures of Articles 93, 169

Over the years, the original concept has been broadened considerably so that the capacity to create direct effects is no longer regarded as something exceptional possessed by only a few special provisions of the Treaty. Rather, it is, in the words of Judge Pescatore, "the normal state of health of the law."[13] The Treaty forms part of the legal order of each member state, and an inherent characteristic of law is that it is applied by courts wherever it is possible to do so.

Two additional developments, both of them also entirely the product of the Court's jurisprudence, call for a brief comment. First, it has been established that it is not only provisions of the Treaty which are capable of producing direct effects. Regulations, directives and decisions adopted by the Community institutions, and agreements entered into by the Community with other states, may also in appropriate circumstances give rise to rights enforceable by individuals in their national courts. The importance of this development can be appreciated when one considers the delays which commonly occur in the implementation of directives and the frequency with which member states are brought before the Court, under Article 169, for failure to implement directives.[14] The directive is the instrument prescribed by the Treaty for attaining many of its stated objectives, and especially for the harmonization of laws, and is thus of particular importance as a means of completing the Internal Market. The fact that, if member states are derelict in their duty to translate directives into provisions of domestic law within the time prescribed, individuals may rely upon the directive in legal proceedings against the state—for example, by refusing to pay a tax which should have been abolished[15]—makes it a far more potent instrument of integration than it would otherwise have been.

Secondly, the court has developed the concept that has come to be known as "horizontal" direct effect. The *Van Gend en Loos* case, as we have seen, was concerned with the question of whether or not an individual could rely upon the Treaty as against a member state which was in breach of the Treaty,

---

and 171. Since a high proportion of the latter concerned failure to implement directives, it is probably fair to say that about 90 percent of rulings on the interpretation of the EEC Treaty and secondary legislation have been delivered in Article 177 cases, and that very few of those references would have been made had it not been for the principle of direct effect.

[13]See note 8 above, p. 155.

[14]Over a seven-year period, 1975–1981, the Commission initiated 1,001 infringement proceedings against member states, of which 66 percent were for nonimplementation: S. KRISLOV, C.-D. EHLERMANN and J. WEILER, Community Policy-Making and Implementation Processes, in M. CAPPELLETTI, *et al., op. cit.*, Book 2, p. 69. Normally, proceedings are commenced only in the more egregious cases of delay.

[15]See Case 8/81, *Becker* [1982], E.C.R. 53.

and the same has been true of the great majority of subsequent cases referred to the Court under Article 177 by national courts. The actual consequence of the principle of direct effect has generally been the non-application of some national rule, at the instance of an individual and normally in proceedings in which the other party is the offending government. This is described as "vertical" direct effect. However, a further question arose as to whether provisions of Community law could also have a "horizontal" effect—that is to say, could they create rights which one individual could enforce against another individual?

It seems to have been assumed from the very beginning that the competition rules, or at least the provision in Article 85 making void certain agreements between undertakings, produced direct legal effects as between individuals.[16] Subsequently, the Court has found that other provisions of the Treaty may also produce horizontal effects; thus, Article 30 may be relied upon to prevent an individual enforcing a patent or trademark right, where to do so would result in a partitioning of the market,[17] and Articles 48, 52 and 57, which forbid discrimination in relation to employment and the provision of services against workers and self-employed persons who are nationals of other member states, are binding not only on states but also on employers, trade associations, professional bodies and the like.[18] And in *Defrenne*—perhaps the most controversial of all the Court's rulings[19]—horizontal effect was extended to Article 119, requiring the application of the principle that men and women should receive equal pay for equal work. The Court's ruling effectively conferred rights upon individuals, enforceable against their employers, which were not dependent upon the introduction of implementing legislation on the part of their national governments.[20] In the *Marshall* case,[21] the Court stopped short of extending horizontal direct effect to directives but, in the more recent *Marleasing* case,[22] it established that, in certain circumstances, even directives may be relied upon against individuals.

---

[16]This assumption was implicit in the first reference made to the Court under Article 177; Case 13/61, *Bosch* [1962], E.C.R. 45.

[17]Case 78/70, *Deutsche Grammophon* [1971], E.C.R. 487; Case 15/74, *Centrafarm* [1974], E.C.R. 1147.

[18]Case 36/74, *Walrave* [1974], E.C.R. 1405; Case 13/76, *Dona* [1976], E.C.R. 1333.

[19]Case 43/75, *Defrenne* [1976], E.C.R. 455.

[20]The consequences of the ruling were potentially so far-reaching that the Court took the exceptional step of restricting the temporal effect of its decision.

[21]Case 152/84, *Marshall* [1986], E.C.R. 723.

[22]Case C 106/89, *Marleasing* (decision of November 13, 1990).

## B. The Supremacy of Community Law

Direct effect ensures that Community law is operative within the legal order of the member states; it does not, of itself, establish the status of Community law within the hierarchy of applicable legal norms, for although the *Van Gend en Loos* case was essentially concerned with the question whether the new Dutch tariff prevailed over the Treaty, the supremacy of the Treaty—once it was established that it had direct effect—was ensured by the provisions of the Dutch constitution itself. The supremacy of Community law over conflicting national law was most clearly articulated in the famous decision in *Costa v. ENEL*,[23] which concerned the validity of Italian legislation adopted after the EEC Treaty had entered into force. The Italian Corte Costituzionale had taken the view that, although the provisions of the Treaty were effective, the earlier obligation must give way to the subsequent law in accordance with the principles governing the succession of laws in time; *lex posterior derogat legi priori*. The Court of Justice, however, ruled that the EEC Treaty had created its own legal order whereby member states had restricted their sovereign rights, with the result that a subsequent unilateral law may not prevail if it is incompatible with the aims of the Community. This principle of supremacy was clearly reaffirmed in a subsequent reference from an Italian court,[24] in which it was ruled that national courts are obliged to set aside any provision of national law that conflicts with Community law, whether prior to or subsequent to the Community rule, even where the national constitutional law permits only the constitutional court of that country to declare a law to be invalid. Community law thus prevails even over national constitutional law.

## C. Preemption and Fundamental Rights

Although the principles of direct effect and supremacy are justly regarded as the cornerstones of the system of Community law, two further principles have been evolved and form important elements in the process of constitutionalization. The doctrine of preemption has been described as "the third hallmark of normative supranationalism,"[25] though its limits have yet to be fully circumscribed.[26] In its purest form the doctrines of direct effect and of

---

[23]Case 6/64, *Costa* [1964], E.C.R. 585.

[24]Case 106/77, *Simmenthal* [1978], E.C.R. 629.

[25]J. WEILER, The Community System: The Dual Character of Supranationalism, *Yearbook of European Law*, 1 (1981), p. 277.

[26]For a penetrating analysis, see M. WAELBROECK, the Emergent Doctrine of Community Preemption—Consent and Re-delegation, in T. SANDALOW and E. STEIN, *Courts and Free Markets*, Oxford, 1982, Book 2, p. 548.

supremacy are taken a stage further; in relation to those areas in which the Community has been given or has assumed policy making competence, the member states are not only precluded from enacting legislation conflicting with Community law but are preempted from taking any action at all. The jurisprudence of the Court provides support for this proposition, at least with respect to the external competence of the Community and of the member states;[27] in purely internal situations the position is less clear.[28] In some instances, national legislation has apparently been struck down because it has trespassed into a field already "occupied" by the Community; in others, on the narrower ground that it is incompatible with existing Community law or established policy in that field.

Since the process of integration is probably not dependent upon the existence of a principle of preemption—although it is no doubt assisted by such a principle—further discussion is not called for here. The same may be said of fundamental rights. Although the EEC Treaty is silent on the matter, the Court has, in a series of decisions,[29] imported into Community law the basic principles of the European Convention on Human Rights. This process, important as it is in the context of the constitutionalization of Community law, is again not central to the process of integration and has relatively little impact upon the completion of the Internal Market, though it will have far greater relevance in the new European Union established by the Maastricht Treaty.[30]

## D. The Role of National Courts in the Constitutionalization Process

The essential consequence of the constitutionalization of Community law is that it is mostly in the national courts that Community law is applied. That is, after all, precisely what is meant by "direct effect." But to be effective,

---

[27]Case 22/70, *Commission v. Council* [1971], E.C.R. 273; Case 41/76, *Donckerwolcke* [1976], E.C.R. 1921. See further, R. BIEBER, On the Mutual Completion of Overlapping Legal Systems: The Case of the European Communities and the National Legal Orders, *European Law Review*, 13 (1988), p. 147; J. TEMPLE LANG, The *ERTA* Judgment and the Court's Case-Law on Competence and Conflict, *Yearbook of European Law*, 6 (1986), p. 183.

[28]Contrast the decisions in Case 31/74, *Galli* [1975], E.C.R. 47; Case 50/76, *Amsterdam Bulb* [1977], E.C.R. 137.

[29]Case 29/69, *Stauder* [1969], E.C.R. 419; Case 11/70, *Internationale Handelsgesellschaft* [1970], E.C.R. 1125; Case 4/73, *Nold* [1974], E.C.R. 491. See further, J. WEILER, Eurocracy and Distrust, *Washington Law Review*, 61 (1986), p. 1103; K. LENAERTS, Fundamental Rights to be Included in a Community Catalogue, *European Law Review*, 16 (1991), p. 367.

[30]See below.

the process necessarily requires the collaboration of the national courts themselves; the principles articulated by the Court of Justice, especially the principle of supremacy, have to be accepted and applied by the courts of the member states. Although this has not been achieved without resistance in some cases,[31] one should not overlook the fact that the courts of the member states have played an active role in the process of constitutionalization.[32] And it is, of course, the national courts that must apply Community law, which can be enforced only by means of national procedures and the remedies that exist under national law.[33]

## III. INTEGRATION THROUGH INTERPRETATION

In establishing Community law as an independent legal order producing individually enforceable rights, the Court possessed *une certaine idée de l'Europe*;[34] this vision seems equally to have guided the Court in its instrumental role in determining the precise contents of those rights. The EEC Treaty itself established the "four freedoms" which constitute the "foundations of the Community"—the free movement of goods, persons, services and capital; the Court, in its role as interpreter of the Treaty, determines the precise extent of those freedoms. In performing this function the Court has consistently adopted the principle of *l'effet utile*; the Treaty should be interpreted in such a way as to promote and attain its stated objectives.[35] One case, the famous ruling in *Cassis de Dijon*,[36] will suffice as an illustration.

---

[31] For example, note the reluctance of French and German courts to accept the direct effect of directives.

[32] For example, note the Belgian Cour d'Appel in *Fromagerie Le Ski* [1970], C.M.L.R. 219.

[33] See J. BRIDGE, Procedural Aspects of the Enforcement of European Community Law Through the Legal Systems of Member States, *European Law Review*, 9 (1984), p. 28; J. STEINER, How to Make the Action Suit the Case, *European Law Review*, 12 (1987), p. 102.

[34] P. PESCATORE, *loc. cit.*

[35] See further, F. DUMON, The Case Law of the Court of Justice: A Critical Examination of the Methods of Interpretation, and C. HAMSON, Methods of Interpretation: A Critical Assessment of Results, in the *Report of the Judicial and Academic Conference*, Luxembourg, 1976.

[36] Case 120/78, *Rewe-Zentrale AG* [1979], E.C.R. 649. Of the abundant literature on this case, see especially A. DASHWOOD, The Cassis de Dijon Line of Authority, in St. J. BATES *et al.* (eds.), *In Memoriam J.D.B. Mitchell*, London, 1983.

The plaintiff in the original proceedings appealed against a refusal by the competent national authority to allow the marketing in Germany of a liqueur imported from France known as "Cassis de Dijon." The refusal was on the basis of a statutory provision that fixed a minimum alcohol content for various categories of drinks. Cassis de Dijon had an alcohol content below the prescribed minimum. The importer alleged that the refusal, and the national legislation upon which it was based, contravened Article 30 of the EEC Treaty and constituted a measure having an effect equivalent to a quantitative restriction on imports from other member states. The question referred to the Court of Justice by the German court was whether legislation such as that fixing minimum alcohol contents for drinks, with the result that traditional products from other member states could not lawfully be marketed, did indeed offend against Article 30.

The Court accepted that, in the absence of common rules on the production and marketing of alcohol, those were matters for the member states to regulate themselves. Accordingly, it ruled:

> Obstacles to movement within the Community resulting from disparities between the national laws relating to the marketing of the products in question must be accepted in so far as those provisions may be recognized as being necessary in order to satisfy mandatory requirements relating in particular to the effectiveness of fiscal supervision, the protection of public health, the fairness of commercial transactions and the defence of the consumer.

That is to say, where obstacles to trade are caused by national rules, those rules can be justified insofar as they serve a legitimate purpose and go no further than is necessary to attain that purpose. But if they cannot be so justified, then they may not be applied by the national court. To quote Professor Dashwood:

> The Court was quite clearly talking about rules that do not discriminate between imports and domestic products but hinder the movement of goods simply because they differ from the relevant rules in the member state of export.[37]

Thus, it is not only rules which discriminate against the products of other member states that are prohibited.[38] In the absence of harmonization, national

---

[37]*Ibid.*, pp. 146–147.

[38]Contrast this with the jurisprudence on freedom of establishment (Article 52) and freedom to provide services (Article 59). In the former case, the prohibition is against discrimination; see Case 221/85, *Commission v. Belgium* [1987], E.C.R. 719. In the case of Article 59. however. the Court has been more inclined to take the

rules must be judged by a standard of reasonableness and will not be permitted unnecessarily to obstruct trade. Not only does this greatly expand the number of situations in which individuals may claim the protection of the Treaty but it also has important implications for the Community's harmonization program. In confirming that national rules which interfere with the proper functioning of the common market are, to that extent, contrary to the Treaty and *ipso facto* non-applicable, it established that it is not necessary to wait until such obstacles are eliminated by way of Community legislation for the harmonization of laws.

This position is consistent with the Court's earlier ruling in *Reyners*.[39] There it had ruled that the prohibition in Article 52 of the EEC Treaty against discrimination on the basis of nationality with respect to the freedom of establishment was an absolute one, once the transitional period provided for in the Treaty had expired, notwithstanding that the Treaty itself envisaged the adoption of directives to secure this freedom. According to the Court:

> The rule on equal treatment with nationals is one of the fundamental legal provisions of the Community. . . . In laying down that freedom of establishment shall be attained at the end of the transitional period, Article 52 thus imposes an obligation to attain a precise result, the fulfillment of which had to be made easier by, but not made dependent on, the implementation of a programme of progressive measures. The fact that this progression has not been adhered to leaves the obligation itself intact beyond the end of the period provided for its fulfillment. . . . After the expiry of the transitional period, the directives provided for by the Chapter on the right of establishment have become superfluous with regard to implementing the rule on nationality, since it is henceforth sanctioned by the Treaty itself with direct effect.

One result of the decision was that the Commission scrapped a number of proposed directives, designed to secure the abolition of discrimination based on nationality, since they had become "superfluous." Henceforth, the task of the Community was seen as one of approximating those (legitimate) provisions of national law, where it was the differences between national rules, rather than the content of any particular rule, which impeded the freedom of establishment or the freedom to provide services.

---

same broad view as with Article 30, and to strike down unreasonable obstacles to the freedom to provide services even when these are not overtly discriminatory.

[39]Case 2/74, *Reyners* [1974], E.C.R. 631.

The effects of the *Defrenne* judgment[40] were essentially similar in nature. The direct effect of Article 119 meant that it was no longer necessary to try to produce Community legislation on equal pay for men and women, since the right to equal pay derived directly from the Treaty itself. The focus consequently shifted to those areas beyond the reach of directly effective Treaty provisions, such as equal access to employment. Similarly, as a result of *Cassis de Dijon*, the Commission's entire strategy towards harmonization of technical standards was revised.[41] National laws which created obstacles to the free movement of goods, and which could not be justified according to the criteria laid down by the Court, had (in theory) become unenforceable; the Commission's work of harmonization would henceforth have to be directed mainly at those national laws impacting upon the common market which were not invalid by virtue of Article 30.

The interpretation by the Court of the precise scope and effect of provisions of the Treaty has three important implications. First, it determines the extent of the rights and obligations that the provision confers on individuals; second, by establishing the extent to which a Treaty provision is effective *without* further enactment, it sometimes also determines those instances where further legislative action *is* necessary in order to achieve the aims of the Treaty; third, since it is axiomatic that provisions of the Treaty which have direct effect cannot be made to depend on a further contingency, such as the adoption of directives,[42] it follows that no derogation by any measure adopted by an institution of the Community will be permitted from a provision of the Treaty which is of a mandatory nature.[43] Secondary legislation adopted by the Council or Commission must be in conformity with the Treaty, and Community regulations, decisions or directives may not sanction a violation of Community law on the part of a member state,[44] or otherwise modify the Treaty.[45]

---

[40]See note 19 above.

[41]Communication from the Commission to the Council, published October 3, 1980: *O.J.*, 1980, C256/2.

[42]Case 168/78, *Commission v. France* [1980], E.C.R. 347; Case 193/80, *Commission v. Italy* [1982], E.C.R. 3015.

[43]Case 15/81, *Gaston Schul* [1982], E.C.R. 1489. In cases of ambiguity the Court will consequently interpret a provision of a directive (or regulation) in a manner which is consistent with the Treaty, if this is possible.

[44]M. WAELBROECK, *loc. cit.*, p. 571, and see Case 59/75, *Manghera* [1976], E.C.R. 91; Cases 80, 81/77, *Commissionnaires Réunis and Ramel* [1978], E.C.R. 927.

[45]Case 12/74, *Commission v. Germany* [1975], E.C.R. 181; Case 24/75, *Petroni* [1975], E.C.R. 1149; Case 46/76, *Bauhuis* [1977], E.C.R. 5.

Consequently, the interpretation that the Court gives to a provision of the Treaty may also have the effect of defining the parameters of any possible legislative effort to give effect to that provision.

The boundaries of legislative competence may thus effectively be determined by the Court. On the one hand, through the exercise of its power to review and to rule upon the validity of Community acts,[46] the Court has power to ensure that where secondary legislation has been adopted it is in accordance with the Treaty. On the other hand, rulings of the Court that interpret the provisions of the Treaty, in situations where no secondary legislation has yet been adopted, may provide an indication of the type of secondary legislation that would conform to the Treaty and may thus preclude certain actions which the Community legislators might otherwise have considered taking.

## IV. COMPLETING THE INTERNAL MARKET: THE ROLE OF COURT AND LEGISLATOR

The preceding sections of this chapter have attempted to illustrate the extent to which the Court of Justice has been responsible for the promotion of integration within the Community. The Treaty has been transformed into a constitution, which has become an essential part of the law applied by the courts in all of the member states. Provisions of the Treaty have been interpreted in such a way as to create meaningful rights, enforceable by citizens in those courts. But even for a court that has sometimes been accused of excessive judicial legislation, there are limits to the extent to which jurisprudence can contribute to the process of integration and the creation of a fully integrated single market in Europe. When those limits are reached, further progress must depend upon the legislators.

It may be significant that the Commission's White Paper, *Completing the Internal Market*,[47] devotes only eight short paragraphs, out of a total of two hundred and twenty-two, to the "Application of Community Law" and that the Court of Justice is not even mentioned in those eight paragraphs. Indeed, only four references to the Court appear in the entire document and in each case the reference is to what the Court has achieved in the past: no specific role was perceived for the Court in the completion of the Internal Market by the 1992 target date. The Court fares somewhat better in the Single European Act,[48] which provides for the creation of a new Court of First Instance to deal with

---

[46]Under Article 173/EEC a direct challenge may be made as to the validity of acts of the institutions. Essentially the same issues may also be brought before the Court by way of requests for preliminary rulings on validity, under Article 177.

[47]White Paper from the Commission to the European Council, June 14, 1985; Doc. COM (85) 310, final.

[48]Single European Act of February 28, 1986, *O.J.* 1987, L 169/1.

certain types of cases. But this seems to have been in response to an already excessive workload rather than to any expectation that the Court would have an additional burden to bear on the road to 1992.

In view of the crucial importance of the role hitherto played by the Court in the process of integration, it must be asked why it seemed to have been given virtually no role in the completion of the Internal Market. Two explanations, which are mutually reinforcing, have been suggested by Judges Pescatore and Koopmans. In his farewell address to the Court,[49] of which he had been a distinguished member for 18 years, Judge Pescatore recalled three distinct phases in the history of the Court. The 1960s was a period of excitement and drama in which the Court issued a series of famous judgments defining the fundamental characteristics of Community law. In the 1970s the Court "defined and refined the legislative system of the Community." But in the 1980s, issues had become infinitely more complex and "the great questions of principle" had been resolved, leaving the Court to deal with a thousand and one problems of a more technical nature. Judge Koopmans, too, identified three phases[50]: institutionalism, instrumentalism and minimalism. During the first decade, the Community legal system was established as a legal order in its own right. The cases of the second phase, the 1970s, generally did not concern institutional problems but dealt rather with the way in which the law can contribute to realizing the general aims of the Treaty. To quote Judge Koopmans, "the Europeans first discovered the importance of law and legal institutions, and then found out how many interesting things you could *do* with the law."[51] But this was followed by a breakdown of legal optimism and a realization that the courts cannot by themselves achieve European integration. As a consequence, the third phase, the 1980s, was marked by a "return to minimalism," or what might perhaps be described as a period of consolidation, in which it is the legal craftsman who is needed more than the visionary or the missionary.

As the end of the 1980s approached, the era of the judge as lawmaker appeared to be largely past. In part this may have reflected a gradual change in the Court's own perception of its role and a collective retreat from judicial activism. Certainly, there have been a few decisions in recent years in which the Court has appeared rather more cautious than might have been the case ten or fifteen years earlier although, as recent decisions in cases such as *Factortame*,[52]

---

[49]Reproduced in *European Law Review*, 11 (1986), p. 3.

[50]T. KOOPMANS, The Role of Law in the Next State of European Integration, *International and Comparative Law Quarterly*, 35 (1986), p. 925.

[51]*Ibid*., p. 928.

[52]Case C 213/89, *Factortame* (decision of June 19, 1990).

*Marleasing*[53] and *Francovich and Bonifaci*[54] demonstrate, the Court is still able and willing to deliver important and controversial judgments. But essentially, it seemed, the major questions of principle had been resolved. The Court had for the most part done all that could be done to secure the conditions which make possible the creation of a genuine Internal Market.[55] Attention would now have to be concentrated upon the legislation which must be adopted in order to complete the Internal Market.

For example, in the case of the free movement of goods, it is thanks to the Court that national measures which discriminate against imported products, or which unreasonably restrict trade, have been outlawed;[56] but there are many cases in which it is the differences between national measures that obstruct the free flow of goods and cause partitioning of the market, without those measures being in any way contrary to Community law. In such cases only harmonization can eliminate the remaining barriers. The Court can establish a rule requiring the mutual recognition of the health and safety standards of member states; it cannot design a plug that ensures that one can use a hair dryer or shaver anywhere within the Community without the use of an adaptor or transformer. Discriminatory taxation can be declared illegal, but the elimination of fiscal frontiers requires not only the abolition of discrimination but also a relatively high degree of uniformity of tax systems and rates—something which can only be achieved by legislation at the Community level.

The Court, in its role of interpreter of the Treaty, can define the task of the legislator. It remains with the legislator to choose the appropriate means of attaining the prescribed objective, subject to the proviso that those means must be consistent with the fundamental principles of Community law as enunciated by the Court.

---

[53]See note 22 above.

[54]Cases C 6, 9/90, *Francovich and Bonifaci* (decision of November 19, 1991).

[55]See P. VERLOREN VAN THEMAAT, The Contributions to the Establishment of the Internal Market by the Case-law of the Court of Justice of the European Communities, in R. BIEBER *et al.* (eds.), *1992: One European Market?*, Baden-Baden, 1988, p. 109.

[56]That is not to say that such measures no longer exist; the number of infraction proceedings brought by the Commission against member states under Article 169 is testimony to their persistence. But such measures can be challenged in the national courts and, if found to offend against Article 30, may not be enforced.

## V. MONETARY AND POLITICAL UNION: THE MAASTRICHT TREATY

The preceding analysis tends to confirm the view that the Court can have only a small role to play in achieving the completion of the Internal Market or, rather, that having played an extremely important role in Acts I and II, it has now departed from centre stage and the other actors—Commission, Council and Parliament—must see the endeavour through to a successful conclusion in Act III. Thus, having progressed through the institutionalist, instrumentalist and minimalist phases, one may ask what is left for the Court to do, other than to deal with scores of questions such as whether Community law permits the date of laying to be indicated on a packet of eggs.[57]

Any idea that the Court is destined to remain restricted to such a minimalist role should be dispelled on examining the Maastricht Treaty. It seems inevitable that, if and when the amendments to the EEC Treaty agreed upon at Maastricht enter into force, the Court will be faced not only with a considerably increased workload but also with a variety of issues of fundamental importance that will determine the nature of the European Union well into the next century.

There are, to begin with, numerous new and complex provisions that will have to be interpreted; those governing the Monetary Union, in particular, are drafted with an imprecision that seems to invite recourse to the Court. Since many of those provisions relate to the extremely sensitive issue of the transfer of control over the main instruments of economic policy from the member states to the Community, the manner in which they are interpreted by the Court will be of particular importance, and is likely to have a major influence upon the pace and intensity of monetary integration. Entire new fields of activity are brought within the sphere of Community concern: culture, education, the environment and public health, hitherto very much peripheral to Community policy, will be brought increasingly under central control. Cooperation in the fields of justice and home affairs will render issues such as immigration, refugee status and the rights of aliens subject to review. The precise scope of the rights and obligations deriving from citizenship of the Union, and from the Social Charter, will call for definition.

New legal principles are introduced and will have to be developed. In addition to the reference, in the Preamble to the Maastricht Treaty, to the *rule of law*, the Treaty expressly incorporates the *fundamental rights* guaranteed by the European Convention on Human Rights. It also incorporates the *principle of subsidiarity* as a basic principle of Community law. This would seem to mean that the Court, in appropriate cases, will have to determine whether actions taken at the Community level might not more appropriately have been left to the

---

[57]Case C 372/89, *Gold-Ei* (decision of January 15, 1991).

member states. The Court is thus confronted with the contentious question of the division of powers. At the same time, the new Articles 171 and 172, which introduce the power to impose sanctions upon member states that fail to comply with judgments of the Court,[58] are likely to have the effect of raising the level of interest, and of controversy, surrounding such judgments.

Finally, the new legislative processes, providing for increased involvement of the Parliament and for greater use of qualified majority voting in the Council, again raise the issue of the division of powers and competences, both as between Community and member states and as between the different institutions of the Community.

In sum, therefore, it seems probable that the next decade will see the Court performing a role no less important than the one played during its institutional and instrumental phases and one that, given the potential subject matter of the questions with which it will be called upon to deal, is likely to be more controversial and to attract greater publicity.

## VI. THE RELATIONSHIP BETWEEN COURT AND LEGISLATOR IN THE NEW EUROPEAN UNION

The importance of law in the process of integration is self-evident. As the editors of the monumental study, *Integration Through Law*, state:

> Integration is not a simple exercise in power sharing, but goes deeper and aims at a fundamental restructuring of society and of societal attitudes, and these changes are reflected in and promoted by the law.[59]

Law is not simply *an* instrument, but is *the* instrument, through which integration is achieved.

In this process, the legislator and the judge play complementary roles. Insofar as the function of the courts is to interpret and apply the laws promulgated by the legislator, the judiciary plays a supporting role; but in that the judiciary may ultimately possess the power to determine what the legislator may or may not do, the legislator may be perceived as an auxiliary, whose task it is to fill in the details of the grand scheme, outlined by the authors of the Treaty—or Constitution—as interpreted by the judges. Usually the courts are more accustomed to playing the supporting role, and it is probably because the European Court has been perceived as so often playing the dominant role that it has attracted so much interest and attention from constitutional scholars.

---

[58]In infraction proceedings brought under Articles 169 and 170.

[59]M. CAPPELLETTI *et al.*, *op. cit.*, pp. 42–43.

To fully appreciate the respective roles of court and legislature it is necessary to consider the dynamics of the Community. On the one hand are what may be termed the external dynamics—the relationship between the central, Community, competence and that of the peripheral member states. On the other are the internal dynamics—the inter-relationship of the Community organs themselves. Until comparatively recently, attention had largely been concentrated upon the Court's participation in the relationship between the Community and member states. Inevitably, comparisons have been drawn with the role of supreme courts in other federal systems; two of the most influential compendia in recent years, *Courts and Free Markets*[60] and *Integration Through Law*,[61] have taken as their main theme such comparisons, and Professor H. Rasmussen's controversial study[62] also draws heavily upon comparative material. Invariably, such studies reveal the Court of Justice to be unusually integrationist, or "federalist."

Undoubtedly, this centrist bias derives in large measure from the Court's own vision of Europe and, for the most part, it has secured the approbation of the critics, most of whom seem to share that vision. But this bias, it is suggested, may be justified on more objective grounds. Generally, in federal systems the supreme or constitutional court is required to hold the balance between central and regional interests. It must strive to preserve the union from disintegration, whilst protecting the constituent members from undue encroachment on the part of the central power. But in the European Community such encroachment is, or has been until very recently, not a real danger. The power to legislate on behalf of the Community has resided almost exclusively with the Council of Ministers, that is to say, with the representatives of the member states themselves, and after the so-called "Luxembourg Accord" of 1966 virtually all important decisions of the Council have, in effect, been taken unanimously.[63] For all practical purposes, therefore, any involuntary incursion upon the legislative territory of a member state has been highly unlikely, if not impossible. In that sense, then, there has been no balance for the Court to maintain. The only danger has been one of disintegration and the dissipation of the *acquis communautaire*, by the improper actions of the member states acting individually, or in concert in the Council, and the Court has thus perforce been

---

[60]M. WAELBROECK, *loc. cit.*

[61]M. CAPPELLETTI *et al.*, *op. cit.*

[62]H. RASMUSSEN, *op. cit.*

[63]It is probably too early to judge the extent to which this practice has been changed by virtue of the Single European Act; see further D. EDWARD, The Impact of the Single Act on the Institutions, *Common Market Law Review*, 24 (1987), p. 19; S. CROSBY, The Single Market and the Rule of Law, *European Law Review*, 16 (1991), p. 451.

cast in a centrist role. This is not to deny, of course, that the Court might have played that role with greater or less vigour and conviction. In determining, for example, that Article 30 of the EEC Treaty prohibits not only those national measures which formally discriminate against the products of other member states, but also those which, while formally neutral, have that effect, and that measures which incidentally have a discriminatory effect offend no less than those which are designed to do so, the Court made positive choices which displayed a centrist bias. Those choices, however, have generally been perceived to have been legitimate ones.

More controversial, at least in recent years, has been the Court's internal, or institutional, role. In particular, as Rasmussen would allege,[64] the Court has become too deeply and too frequently involved in the political government of the Community and has, in effect, usurped the role of the legislator. As Rasmussen states

> . . . the Court of Justice's lawmaking activities, defiant of much European tradition in that respect, were regularly preceded by deep involvements in making choices between competing public policies for which the available sources of law did not offer the Court judicially applicable guidelines.

Thus, in cases such as *Reyners*[65] and *Defrenne*,[66] the Treaty clearly envisaged action on the part of the legislature to secure the abolition of discrimination with regard to the freedom of establishment, and to promote equal pay for men and women, yet the Court was prepared to circumvent such action, or compensate for legislative inaction, by declaring Articles 52 and 119 to have direct effect. In the opinion of Rasmussen, these are cases of "blatant and unacceptable activism."[67]

Here again, however, the activism of the Court has to be viewed in the context of the institutional structure of the Community and the legislative paralysis which it has engendered. Certainly, the Court has on many occasions assumed the role of legislator,[68] but frequently this is not so much because the

---

[64]H. RASMUSSEN, p. 508. For comprehensive critiques of Rasmussen's analysis, see M. CAPPELLETTI, Is the European Court of Justice "Running Wild"?, *European Law Review*, 12 (1987), p. 3; J. WEILER, The Court of Justice on Trial, *Common Market Law Review*, 24 (1987), p. 555.

[65]See note 39 above.

[66]See note 19 above.

[67]H. RASMUSSEN, *op. cit.*, p. 29.

[68]Professor Cappelletti would prefer to describe the judges as "lawmakers," rather than as "legislators"; M. CAPPELLETTI, The Law-making Power of the Judge

Court has usurped the proper function of the legislator, but rather because the legislator has failed to act where action has been necessary and required by the Treaty. If the Court has become too deeply involved in making choices between competing policies, it is primarily because the Council has been unable or unwilling to make those choices. In the great majority of cases in which the Court has assumed the role of legislator, the alternatives have not been action by the Court or action by the Council, but rather action by the Court or inaction. Indeed, one can go further and suggest that the real alternatives have been action by the Court or the non-observance of the Treaty itself, bringing into disrepute the entire fabric of Community law. In such circumstances, usurpation seems preferable to disintegration.

The increased resort to majority voting in the Council and the enhanced participation of the Parliament in the legislative process, begun by the Single European Act and continued in the Maastricht Treaty, should greatly reduce the risk of legislative paralysis. If in future the institutions do not act, that inaction may simply be the expression of a democratically taken decision not to act. There should consequently be less occasion, and less justification, for the Court to impose what are in effect legislative solutions.

At the same time, the new legislative procedures must inevitably give rise to disputes involving questions of procedure and competence. This is especially so since different procedures apply for different types of measures. In some cases unanimity in the Council is still required; in others a qualified majority will suffice. Sometimes it is only necessary to consult the Parliament; in other cases, it is given a more substantial role in the legislative procedure, with powers of revision and rejection.[69] The choice of the appropriate basis for Community legislation may not always be an obvious one, yet that choice may determine the respective competences of Parliament and the Council,[70] or whether the Council must act unanimously or by a qualified majority.[71] Questions of this nature have arisen already under the existing Treaty, especially since its amendment by the Single European Act,[72] but the disputes have been

---

and Its Limits: A Comparative Analysis, *Monash University Law Review*, 8 (1981), p. 42. That is to say, legislatures and judges both have a part in the creation of the law. But in a real sense, Professor Rasmussen's charge that the Court of Justice has acted as legislator seems justified, if perhaps over-stated.

[69]See the new Articles 189, 189b and 189c, inserted by the Maastricht Treaty.

[70]Case C 70/88, *Parliament v. Council* (decision of May 22, 1990); see K. LENAERTS, *loc. cit.*

[71]Case 68/86, *United Kingdom v. Council* [1988], E.C.R. 855; Case C 300/89, *Commission v. Council* (decision of July 11, 1991). See further S. CROSBY, *loc. cit.*

[72]See notes 70 and 71 above.

more in the nature of preliminary sparring in order to establish certain positions; the complainant institution or member state has generally not objected to the substance of the disputed measure but only to its juridical basis and the procedure by which it was adopted.

However, it seems inevitable that the time will come when legislation is adopted, or purports to be adopted, to the substance of which a member state or institution takes strong exception. The validity of the measure will be challenged, either on the ground that it was incorrectly based upon a particular provision of the Treaty or that it offends against the principle of subsidiarity. The Court will then find itself cast in the position, more familiar to federal constitutional courts, of holding the balance between central and regional interests.[73] The result could be a fundamental change in the role of the Court.

---

[73]See further, J.-P. JACQUÉ and J.H.H. WEILER, On the Road to European Union: A New Judicial Architecture, *Common Market Law Review*, 27 (1990), p. 185; K. LENAERTS, *loc. cit*.

# REAPPRAISING THE ORIGINS OF EUROPEAN INTEGRATION*

Pierre-Henri LAURENT
*Tufts University*

Now that the "post post-war" period has been announced, there may be some greater value in assessing the integration movement of Europe in the time that David Calleo has called "the founding cycle."[1]

The historiography of post-war European-American relations falls into two chronological categories. First, there are those studies on the initial period of labors to create regional or transnational institutions from 1945 to the creation of the EEC in 1958. Second, there are the works on the period since that time which are primarily about the European Community itself. This twofold distinction is based on the increasingly large number of diverse interpretive studies of the forties and fifties with their heavy reliance on substantial and recently released primary sources. The second body of literature is characterized by its relatively small number of *historically* oriented works and the paucity of significant primary historical sources.

This article examines and analyzes representative production of the first group only. Although there are some exceptions, the historical content, especially the historical analysis, of post-1960 literature is scanty and any study of it for telling commonalities, patterns, relationships, etc., is not at this time highly productive. The writings that are covered herein are the end result of efforts by both historians and social scientists whose primary goal was setting forth the historical events of European integration and then interpreting them. This combining of the historical approach and analytical method that seeks to determine first-stage integration causality becomes the nexus of this exploration.

The analysis of the first cycle in integration literature yields up not just the existence of potent European concerns about their future economic viability, but the centrality of certain new economic and political goals among the national leaders. Beyond the Cold War pressures and the general impetus to economic rationalization and modernization, many of the Western Europe elite advocated

---

*This is a revised version of an article that first appeared in Revue d'integration européenne/Journal of European Integration, vol. XII, nos. 2–3 (1989), pp. 101–119.

[1] D. CALLEO, *Beyond American Hegemony: The Future of the Western Alliance*, New York, 1987.

extensive federalist and supranationalist (read radical) resolutions to their problems. One cannot deny that the anti-Red motive which much of the West shared by early 1948 became mingled with this developing pro-integrationist sentiment. But what can now be asserted is that it took, in addition to the apprehension about communism, the creation and existence of an incipient and home-grown unity movement and regional economic collaboration in Europe to produce the transnationalism of that era.

This review of the critical works attempts to demonstrate the genesis and evolution of a European elite conviction about the *sine qua non* of *starting anew*. The outlines of a new multilateralist doctrine and some concrete institutions for collective action can be traced in that first decade. The breed of leaders who proclaimed the indispensable and requisite nature of uniting the fragmented energies and capabilities of the separate, small national economies into one competitive economic superpower became the cardinal actors in integration history. In part, aided by the Americans and threatened by the Soviets, the majority of the continental leadership perceived an economic/technological challenge that necessitated, even forced, a change in their international relations structure. Simply put, the advent and then expansion of mass production and consumption called for economies and markets of scale based on concepts of rapid growth and higher productivity. Narrow and limited national economies within Europe would not be able to survive as major international trade powers unless they organized and practiced effective joint economic actions. The ruinous national rivalry of the past required diplomatic and institutional revision that would allow Western Europe to compete as a major force in the post-war trade system.

Debates about the proper route for these collaborative-collective economic goals (the federalist *versus* functionalist controversy) were immediately evident, but the European idea that economic unification was necessary for Europe's future burst forth from within the Little Europe Six of 1948-58. In the end, as Dirk Stikker said, "economic and military reasons [combined with] . . . political necessity in calling for European unity."

In examining the impulses or causes behind integration, fear of the new threat—communism—was mixed with worry about the old problem—Germany. And significantly, these two forces existed alongside the *indigenous* urge to reorder the economic essentials of the region in adjustment to new compelling global facts. Fusions of national interests were to become the order of the day, for the logic of cooperation, let alone of economic integration, was seen as inexorable. The numerous dedicated and vocal European statesmen, most converted shortly after the war, were already extolling the reasons for a New Europe. Since these initial maneuvers behind and within BENELUX, OEEC, the Council of Europe, ECSC and EPU are now more fully described and understood, they are in large part seen as regional policies and institutions originated by Europeans for their own future well-being, not responses to American urging or possible Soviet expansion. The elitist drive to integrate (from its calls for customs unions, sector supranationality, and even milder joint coordination or harmonization) was therefore not separate from and extraneous to the Cold War pressures, German dilemma and small states' impotence, but a rapidly established proclivity among influential Europeans to regain economic influence and power. It combined with and blended into the mix of variables that conditioned global interactions, but the power-retention rationale behind the integration drive appears to have been foremost for the continentals of that era.

The origins of the first integration period has rapidly become an exciting series of historiographical debates. In something more than a quarter century, but sufficient time for the appearance of several historical generations, historical scholarship has exposed numerous facets of the primary integrationist ideas and actions in Europe. With growing intensity and more thoroughness in the last decade, this research has been broadened and deepened to encompass both the extra-European (primarily superpower) and internal European (both continental and non-continental) forces which worked to bring about either real transfers of power or to coordinate more closely the policies of nations and to institutionalize their policy management. Thus, the understanding and insights are of both the federators and functionalists and even beyond, into the ranks of those who sought to add new regional, multilateral cooperation or unity to the Western European relationships. Even the literature that documents the continuing power of national sovereignty (e.g., Great Britain) in part supports the early successes of integration institutions.

In general, this literature reflects four fairly distinct perspectives. The preponderant school, both in volume and influence until very recently, addresses the pan-European efforts as by-products of the new superpower emergence and the Cold War rivalry. Another group of historians focuses on the paramount role (albeit often but not always negative for integration) of the British. The final two bents on integration share a belief that *internal* Western European imperatives drove the integration process, but they differ essentially on the specifics of causation within the continent and the paramount role of indigenous European integration ideas and actors. This last group has accentuated the conflictual nature of the European-American connection in this founding period, mostly as a consequence of partial differing means and goals on economic integration and the asymmetrical character in the security arena. More frequently over time, since the early sixties and with rapidity in the eighties, many of these more linear historical points of view have been synthesized by some historians into multicausal interpretations.

The apparent overriding determinism of the Soviet-American clash in the first post-war decade has been compelling for many students of early European regionalism experiments. In most cases emanating from American pens, whose preoccupation was comprehending either American foreign policy evolution or the causes of the superpower hostility, these visions by traditionalists like H. Feis, W. McNeil and N. Graebner perceived the US not just as the external federator of Europe, but the primary catalyst of both the ideas and even institutions of the actual European unity movement.[2] As far as European questions were concerned, even the later revisionist school of Americanists like W.A. Williams, G. Kolko and W. Lefeber were uniform and similar in their contention that bipolarity strongly conditioned and/or created the European possibilities and opportunities.[3]

There is, however, in historiographical terms a major distinction to emphasize between these two orientations. The classical Cold War theorists pronounced the apparent westward expansionist policy of the Soviets, if not in 1945, at least by late 1947, as the central cause of the end of the wartime allies and resultant East-West split. This posture resulted in a more heavy focus on *extra*-Europe factors and, in the question of integration, an explanation that stressed Russia as the negative external federator and the US as the benevolent external federator. The revisionists, however, saw an American design at work in Europe which was consistent in its economic and commercial desire to at least influence strongly, if not control, Europe. These historians who highlighted the American will to power were forced to follow their logic into a search for the substance of European reaction and response to their American allies. It is this first stage Americanization of Europe that has historiographically opened the door to the relationship of American ideas and policies and European notions and actions on integration. This probe into "resurgent neocorporatist" Europe, with its free market capitalism center, has moved the previously singular glance of integration historians into the "European dimension." First the work of C. Maier and later D. Hogan highlighted the transfer and interchange of economic and political thinking across the Atlantic in which American entrepreneurs and state officials tried to encourage Europe to emulate the competitive liberal capitalism of the US.[4] The appearance of the notion that the Europeans extolled and praised *capital* which was different from the American belief and commitment in *capitalism* has led to numerous insights that deny the unanimity of outlook and motivation in the Western bloc.

Historical comprehension about the security aspects of post-war Europe, which has been covered and explained better than the economic aspect, has been based, until recently, on the formation of an early Atlanticist

---

[2]H. FEIS, *Churchill, Roosevelt, Stalin: The War They Waged and the Peace They Sought*, Princeton, 1957; W. McNEIL, *America, Britain and Russia: Cooperation and Conflict*, Chicago, 1953; and N. GRAEBNER, *Cold War Diplomacy*, Princeton, 1961.

[3]W.A. WILLIAMS, *The Tragedy of American Diplomacy*, New York, 1960; G. KOLKO, *The Limits of Power: The World and United States Foreign Policy*, New York, 1972; and W. LEFEBER, *America, Russia and the Cold War*, New York, 1976.

[4]C. MAIER, *In Search of Stability*, Cambridge, 1988; and D. HOGAN *The Marshall Plan*, Cambridge, 1987.

consensus, more recent American students and many Europeans of the strategic sphere have demonstrated the disparate, even factious, nature of transatlanticism and the fragmentation represented by 1954. Even though a fuller dislodgement of the common security consensus occurred only in the sixties with de Gaulle, much newer literature demonstrates the earlier divisions over the basic nature and structure of military integration. There, the correlation between the findings on Euro-American security studies and European integration increasingly appears to grow, with common threads in the *limited* consensus and the early *divergences* within the West on the motives behind and means to be used on major security *and* economic issues. This conclusion does not deny that the Europeans preferred outright American hegemony and were basically enthusiastic about America in charge of NATO. What it means is Europeans in many cases wished to borrow both American ideas and power in order to apply them to either their *own* national interests and goals or to their collective purpose of a regional economic *reliance*, or both.[5]

The US-USSR domination centerpiece has long prescribed that Western Europe was the "passive victim of superpower politics," as David Reynold so aptly and succinctly put it.[6] This historical perception saw the American reordering and then rebuilding of devastated Europe as determining the form, shape and even timing of any "new Europe." Even the thinking behind integration had its origin in the minds of Americans. The all-powerful galvanizing agents for European change were, it was said, the menace of the Soviets and the friendly notions and capital of the Americans. Again, critical to the transformation of integration scholarship was the revisionist deviation that American political, strategic and economic motives, essentially the interventionist posture, were dominant over European economic needs between 1947 and 1958, clearly reflecting the supremacy of politics and ideology in the then-US position over the European economic future outlook. This belief caused some of these researchers to delve into Western European sources in a much more comprehensive sense, while other similarly inclined colleagues pressed their explorations in depth into the American foreign economic policy formation process. The former group discovered elements of *native* European integration thought and activity; the latter group found some evidence that there was, in reality, a relative absence of truly concerted design or overall plans in US economic policy on Europe.

It is important to note that parallel in time to these historical studies specializing in foreign policy analysis, another small group of students studied

---

[5]See D. CALLEO, *op. cit.* and L. KAPLAN, *NATO and the United States*, Boston, 1988, also KAPLAN's valuable "The Cold War and European Revisionism," *Diplomatic History*, 11, 2 (1987), pp. 143–156.

[6]D. REYNOLDS, "The Origins of the Cold War: The European Dimension, 1944-51," *The Historical Journal*, 28, 2, pp. 497–515.

integration *both* from "within and without." Stressing the internal components of pre-Common Market regional activities were the initial monographs in the sixties by H. Schmitt, F.R. Willis, E. Benoit and E. Van der Beugel.[7] Although produced literally on the heels of the events they studied, most have stood the test of time exceedingly well, primarily because they unearthed the first concrete European documentation, including oral sources, concerning not just *soi-disant* union plans, but wider regional diplomacy. The significance of Schmitt and Willis, for example, was their interpretations based on solid European evidence that the federalist ECSC experiment was at the heart of the Franco-German *rapprochement* and specifically that integration was the tool for resolving the old hostility. These studies furthermore delineated the relationship between political reconciliation and economic integration; the Franco-German *entente* was achieved through the economic avenue and was the idea of a group of Europeans named Monnet, Schuman, Uri, etc.

Again, in roughly the same time span of the sixties, some Britons (and a few continentals) began to take note of their own nations' self-exclusion from the "Europeanist" experiments. Others, recognizing the first expressions of deviance within the new Community (particularly de Gaulle the "inhibitor," as Gerhard Mally put it),[8] ploughed the evidence and found the UK to have been a kind of lynch pin in integration. Acting as an internal inhibitor, British resistance to early integration in fact gave strength to the creation and development of a continental integration consensus, at least amongst the elites. M. Camps, J. Pinder, D. Calleo, N. Beloff, and M. Harrison represented the "widening spectrum" search that emphasized the role of British domestic and global politics in continental integration.[9] These works illuminated the

---

[7]H. SCHMITT, *The Path of European Union*, Baton Rouge, 1962; F.R. WILLIS, *France, Germany and the New Europe, 1945–1967*, Stanford, 1968; E. BENOIT, *Europe at Sixes and Sevens*, New York, 1961; and E. VAN DER BEUGEL, *From Marshall Plan to Atlantic Partnership*, New York, 1966.

[8]R. GRIFFITHS, La Dinamica della Politica d'Inerzia: La partecipazione del Regno Unito ai negoziati di Spaak e il suo successivo ritiro, in E. SERRA, *Diplomazia e storia delle relazioni internazionali*, Roma, 1991; A.G. HARRYVAN and A.E. KERSTEN in the Serra collection; P.-H. LAURENT, Beneluxer Economic Diplomacy and the Creation of Little Europe, 1945-50, *Journal of European Integration*, 10, 1 (1986), pp. 23–38, and America's Ally and Britain's Opponent: Belgium and the OEEC/EPU Debates, *Journal of International Studies*, 26, 3 (1988), pp. 453-67; M. DUMOULIN, *La construction européenne en Belgique*, Louvain, 1988; O. DE RAEYMACKER (ed.), *Small Powers in Alignment*, Leuven, 1974; A. MANNING in POIDEVIN, *op. cit.*; R. RANIERI in K. SCHWABE (ed.), Die Anfänge des Schuman Plans, 1950–51, Baden-Baden, 1988 and the insightful synthesis in G. LUNDESTAD, *The American "Empire,"* Oxford, 1990.

[9]M. CAMPS, *Britain and the European Community, 1955–63*, Princeton, 1964; J. PINDER, *Britain and the Common Market*, London, 1961; D. CALLEO, *op. cit.*; N. BELOFF, *The General Says No*, London, 1966; and M. HARRISON, *The*

divergent set of continental orientations and the West European schism of the 1947–57 era as based much more on internal integration conflicts among Europeans than the broader East-West issues. Again, the evidence is that for Europe the center and not periphery came first.

It required, however, the emergence of the post-revisionist Americanists and "New Europe" European specialists to alter once again the historical landscape on integration. The probings into the separate European paths to and away from integration and the altered judgments about America's role were integral parts in the further dissection of the European dimension. The turning points have been fourfold: the new definition of London's influential role, the revised depiction of the relationship of the "German problem" and France's turn to "Little Europe" leadership, the paradox for Europeans in the Atlantic and European perspectives, and finally the proven existence of fairly independent *European* decisions to resolve *European* issues for *European* reasons.

The result of recently opened archives, particularly the British and some Western European, but also American state papers, and the insights derived from reexamination and reanalysis of older documents, these newest historical interpretations emphasized the nature, actions, and impact of the internal federators. Without in most cases denying the obvious impact of external pressures, these histories bared the internal (both national and cross-national) forces that operated in European public and private politics and economics. Delving into the rise of a novel European identity and direction, these historians frequently assessed new British sources, the private papers, memoirs, and diaries of continental notables plus the materials of political parties and "Europeanist" interest groups. The hegemonic thesis of Soviet-American domination as the prime cause of integration was severely dented.

The most recent historiography has questioned the idea that positive US influence either created or at least accelerated the unification process in Europe. Some historians contended that the American design was the withholding of its power and its contribution that resulted in the delay of integration. Evidence that European unity was not an end in itself for the Americans and that Atlantic Europe was central to them is irrefutable. Not only was Washington's attitude toward Europe more ambivalent, it thought in terms of leadership more than partnership in defense matters and strong client and not formidable competitor in the economic realm.

The hypothesis that the Marshall Plan was very rapidly changed into a Cold War by NATO and NSC-68 that impeded, not simply aided, European cooperation over European concerns has been derived from the inspection of continental thoughts and actions at mid-century. If one moves from an American-assisted recovery *via* ERP to an American-run protectorate and

---

*Reluctant Ally: France and Atlantic Security*, Baltimore, 1981. See also R. McGEEHAN, *The German Rearmament Question: American Diplomacy and European Defense after World War II*, Urbana, 1971.

American-directed NATO and MSA, then the fifties saw the evaluation of not only European resentment about impotence and dependency but a collective desire to work for a future economic self-reliant world strength. In the military sphere, the hegemony reality (clothed in unilateral and pluralistic language) might have to be accepted grudgingly and temporarily. But to accept the limited, and often externally directed, recovery goal became unacceptable to those who believed collective self-sufficiency and an economic bloc of their own could be the route to viable participation in the new international political economy.

European initiatives and drives to foster and control integration are now evident and documented as early as the late forties. To overcome European difficulties began to mean that Europeans viewed their problems with variations on the American theme. They also participated in making collective decisions about Europe's future. If the ferment of Western European integration dynamism is seen by most as early as mid-century, this change is significant because it suggests the possibility of moving the American influence in the formative stage to the *facilitator*, not originator role. Thus, the most recent literature focuses strongly on the 1940-58 integration movement as driven more by self-defined European economic goals and less by American diplomatic goals (traditionalists' point of view) or economic benefits (the revisionists' perspective).

In the results of Americans looking at Europe, the works of C. Maier on American ideas exported to and accepted by Europe, I. Wexler on the Marshall Plan, T. Ireland, M. Harrison and A. Grosser on NATO, J. Gimbel on Berlin and R. Pollard and R. Best on the British still reflected mostly the American dominance and European dependence viewpoint.[10] And yet, these same works found reason in the now fuller and more extensive data of British and continental papers and sources to comment on how soon divisions and differences emerged in the Western alliance camp. What Roy Ginsberg has termed "allied rivalry" is the discovery that what originally appeared to bring the Americans and Western Europeans together was both, in part, myth and also a reality quickly beginning to unravel.

---

[10]C. MAIER *op. cit.*, I. WEXLER, *The Marshall Plan Revisited*, Westport, 1983; T. IRELAND, *Creating the Entangling Alliance*, London, 1981; M. HARRISON, *op. cit.*; A. GROSSER, *The Western Alliance*, London, 1980; J. GIMBEL *The Origins of the Marshall Plan*, Stanford, 1976; R. POLLARD, *Economic Security and the Origins of the Cold War*, New York, 1985; and R. BEST, *Co-operation with Like-Minded Peoples*, Westport, 1986. Two most recent studies in the nineties deal with the linkage between Europe's unification process and the Atlantic alliance, with both stressing the evolving differences of the Western European and American motivations. See W.C. CROWNELL, *The United States and the European Pillar*, New York, 1992; and F.H. HELLER and J.R. GILLINGHAM (eds.), *NATO: The Founding of the Atlantic Alliance and the Integration of Europe*, New York, 1992, in particular the articles of KAPLAN, VAN DER HARST, FOOT, SCHWABE, SCHWARTZ, FURSDON, MILWARD, SORENSEN and ABELSHAUSER plus the GILLINGHAM introduction.

The new historical bent of these American scholars has not been as telling as the findings of the "New Europe" integrationist historians. Starting with the more generalized and earlier works of P. Melandri, J.-B. Duroselle and K. Schwabe, one can see the common thread of weighty European concepts about regional cooperation resulting in a diplomacy of transnational institution building.[11] Yet the big breakthroughs in this school have been the studies of W. Lipgens, and W. Loth, A. Bullock, P. Gerbet, R. Poidevin and his associates, and particularly, A. Milward and some of his students.[12] There is also a major non-Western study emanating from East Germany that gave co-equal status to the integrationists in Europe along with superpower politicians in explaining the construction of European unity.[13] These are all frontier-breaking views because they document aspects of early European individuality, assertiveness and independence. They also share an accentuation on the clear-cut elitist nature of post-war integrationist thinking and politics, and the specific substantive basis of the federalist rivalry within the integrationist elite itself. The degree to which the "high politics" of the integrationist government elite functioned in an increasingly informal alliance with *non*-governmental vested interest groups is best demonstrated in Lipgens and Loth.

The originality and imagination of these statesmen with their visions of a regional bloc with economic change for ultimate political goals comes through markedly in these contributions. Diverse motivations may have existed for these men, but they shared the belief that it was time for larger loyalties than the nation-state. The concerns and considerations of European recovery and reorganization therefore have been subjected to a more intense microscope, and the most current findings demonstrate that plans and planning for Europe were the consequences of the immediate setting and actors at the "center," not those at the "periphery" of Europe or the Atlantic system.

---

[11]P. MELANDRI, *Les États-Unis face a l'unification de l'Europe*, 1945–54, Paris, 1980; J.-B. DUROSELLE, *Histoire diplomatique de 1919 à nos jours*, Paris, 1986 and *France and the United States: From the Beginning to the Present*, Chicago, 1976; K. SCHWABE in R. POIDEVIN (ed.), *Histoire des débuts de la construction européenne, mars 1984-mai 1950*, Bruxelles, 1986.

[12]W. LIPGENS, *A History of European Integration, 1945–47*, Vol. 1, Oxford, 1982; *Documents on the History of European Integration*, Vol. I, Berlin, 1986; W. LOTH, *Documents on the History of European Integration*, Vol. II, Berlin, 1988; A. BULLOCK, *Ernest Bevin: Foreign Secretary 1945–51*, London, 1983; P. GERBET, La genèse du Plan Schuman, *Revue française de science politique*, (1956), pp. 529–307; P. POIDEVIN (ed.), *op. cit.;* A. MILWARD, *The Reconstruction of Western Europe, 1945–51*, Berkeley, 1984; and the forthcoming work by his student, R. RANIERI.

[13]See M. KOLLING, *Führungmacht in West Europa? Grossbritanniens Auspruch und Scheitern, 1944–50*, Berlin, 1984.

The "Europeanness" of the reorganization of Europe's political economy after the war even has historical components that emphasize wartime (mostly London governments-in-exile) activities.[14] But the majority of scholarship that describes the specifics of self-generated European integrationist sentiments and maneuvers concerns the leadership elites of the forties and fifties. In the federalist-functionalist discourse and struggle, most vivid in the Lipgens and Milward volumes, we see a general context of American- and British-led Atlanticism with continental support. The new European ventures, with at minimum goals of cooperation and intergovernmentalism and at maximum unity and supranationalism, were *European* in origin and development and evolved according to regional and national *economic* requirements. The "Little Europe" formation on the continent fused two basic elements—the French-led search for security and a *rapprochement* with a new Germany, and economic integration as a means of reattaining global economic power for Western Europe. Europe should not be ready and willing to simply follow the American lead, so went its argument. Even if the United States were powerful enough to lead the anti-communist defense of the West and strong enough to impose its idea of a new economic order, the Europeans displayed a certain lack of willingness to accede to long-term US dominance in the competitive world trade of tomorrow. Multilateral regional diplomacy aimed at Europe's reconstruction but, more essentially, reorganization became motivated by longer range goals of trade expansion, global liquidity, and European international competition.

Here, the American ideas about economic and political stabilization and the conversion to rapid growth economies based on accelerated productivity appear to have been imported and accepted by the Europeans by 1950.[15] The

---

[14]Three conferences at the University of Hull (U.K.) in the late eighties examined the historical origins of integration. The first two on the interwar and wartime years have been published (see P.M.R. STIRK (ed.), *European Unity in Context*, London, 1989; and M.L. SMITH and P.M.R. STIRK (eds.), *Making the New Europe*, London, 1990). The third on the post–1945 period is due out in late 1992.

[15]The most recent illustrations of the "Euro-centered motivations thesis" are in the work of J. GILLINGHAM, *Coal, Steel and the Rebirth of Europe, 1945–55*, Cambridge, 1991; S. GEORGE, *An Awkward Partner: Britain in the European Community*, New York, 1990; J.W. FRIEND, *The Linchpin: French-German Relations, 1950–1990*, New York, 1991; and C. HACKETT, *Cautions Revolution: The European Community Arrives*, New York, 1990. The Commission of the European Community, directly and indirectly, is responsible for much of this and other recent scholarship with both the releasing of its documents and its conferences that feature numerous eyewitnesses of the 1945-58 period. In particular, see Commission des Communautés Européennes, *Inventaire des Archives Historiques: Dossiers de la Haute Autorité de la CECA 1952*, Luxembourg, 1985; for the original documents, see also K. SCHWABE (ed.), *op. cit.*, for twenty-three articles that utilize such documentations. On the later mid-fifties, see E. SERRA (ed.), *Il Rilancio dell'Europa e i trattati di Roma*, Milano, 1989, with its twenty-one articles. The Schwabe and Serra collections contain many English language works, with the

politics of productivity, as Maier has outlined them, were not insidious American capitalism intervening into Europe, but Europeans enamored with American prescriptions and their application to Europe.

Perhaps the most far-reaching statement on European integration self-determination has been Milward's, *The Reconstruction of Western Europe*. Here is a double thesis, one demonstrating and asserting "the institutionalized patterns of economic interdependence" growing in the Europe of 1945-51 and the second elaborating on the failure of American policy up against European realities in the same period. The current state of the art on integration history is too frequently simplified to a controversy between Milward and, for instance, Maier and Hogan, but the reality is more complex. Milward's great contribution is his depiction of the diversity of needs and the resolutions of the various national reconstruction projects. His portrait of the American projection of its power abroad and unique methods for conquering Europe's ills is one where frequent contrary European interests and inclinations emerge.

Another influence in the furthering of a more complete portrait of the birth and take-off of European integration have been the case studies of the "new British" school, *à la* E. Barker, J. Young, R. Ovendale, J.S. Newton, T. Anderson and primarily the A. Bullock treatment of Bevin and the admirable A. Carew study on *Labour under the Marshall Plan*.[16] The common theme goes beyond fascination with London doings and goes into diverse illustrations of the criticality of British decisions for the continentals. One finds the absence of unanimity beyond regional security cooperation in issues such as sovereignty *vs.* supranationality in the Council of Europe, OEEC/EPU diplomacy and the

---

following of "revisionist" significance: Griffiths, Poidevin, Lynch, Bullen, Kersten, Ranieri, Gillingham, and Milward in the former, and Harryvan and Kersten, Kusters, and Griffiths-Asbeck-Brusse in the latter. In addition, the Serra collection has debates between the "survivor" participants that are extremely valuable because many have not written on their involvement or released their private papers. For another publication that again provides firsthand oral history, see COMMISSION DES COMMUNAUTÉS EUROPÉENNES, *Un Avenir a construire ensemble*, Luxembourg, 1991. See also D. BRINKLEY and C. HACKETT (eds.), *Jean Monnet: The Path to European Unity*, New York, 1991. There is no question that the 30 year law release of national or state papers, including primarily the British and American, have helped the researchers of forties and fifties to be more perceptive scholars in the eighties and nineties.

[16]E. BARKER, *The British Between the Super Powers, 1945–51*, London, 1983; J. YOUNG, *Britain, France and the Unity of Europe, 1945-51*, Leicester, 1984; R. OVENDALE (ed.), *The Foreign Policy of the British Labour Government, 1945–51*, Leicester, 1984, and *The English-Speaking Alliance*, London, 1985; J.S. NEWTON, 1949 Sterling crisis and British Policy toward European Integration, *Review of International Studies*, 1985, pp. 160–182; T. ANDERSON, *The United States, Great Britain and the Cold War, 1944–47*, Columbia, 1981; and A. BULLOCK, *op. cit.*

making of the ECSC and EEC. In fact, the central European issue of Germany at mid-century caused the continentals to not simply accept integration means and ends for security reasons, but to give the Marshall West Europe leaders a legitimacy and broader appeal in the general populace for both domestic political reasons and some desired innovative economic ends. To put it another way, integration may have appealed to European national leaders because it could serve certain significant *national* political ends in their now-broadened constituencies.[17]

The growth of historiographical caution and even skepticism about the American role in integration is most vividly seen in the Milward and Carew monographs. Milward talks about intentions behind the ERP; Carew describes and analyzes what transpired in industrial relations under the Plan. Added to the Hogan study, these reinterpretations present the Western European powers disagreeing with the US ideas of integration, particularly its primary political goals over economic ones. This is illustrated in the militarization of the ECA via the Mutual Security Agency by 1951, which these Europeanists, particularly Carew, insist projected a politically and ideologically oriented American managerialism that many in Europe then rejected or at least criticized. The American methods of management and the accompanying promotion of American enterprise abroad were seen as in conflict with European ideas and even not successful when applied in several national case studies. Carew's judgment that the ERP aid was marginal, created conflict and probably produced questionable deflationary policies may require further studies, but it poses problems about ERP, MSA and their meanings to the Europeans which historians must address.

This *melange* of interconnected European schemes for extensive economic, if not political, restructuring included a pivotal awareness of the impotence of all Europe's national economies in the post-war globe. Probably small state in origin and first visible in wartime London, the belief that a cardinal imperative was the recreation of European competitive capability is at the heart of the depictions of R. Griffiths, A.G. Harryvan and A.E. Kersten, P.-H. Laurent, M. Dumoulin, O. de Raeymacker, A. Manning, R. Ranieri and especially G. Lundestad.[18] Although in one sense clients of the Americans,

---

[17] S. ROMANO in D. ELLWOOD (ed.), *The Marshall Plan Forty Years After: Lessons for the International System Today,* Johns Hopkins SAIS Bologna Center, 1988.

[18] B. ZEEMAN, in his forthcoming monograph on NATO and the three Lowlands states; P.-H. LAURENT, Beneluxer Economic Diplomacy and the Creation of Little Europe, 1945-50, *Journal of European Integration*, 10, 1 (1986), pp. 23–38; O. de RAEYMACKER (ed.), *Small Powers in Alignment*, Leuven, 1974; G. LUNDESTAD, Empire by Invitation: The United States and Western Europe, 1945–51, *SHAFR Newsletter*, 15 (1984), pp. 1–21; and A. MANNING in POIDEVIN, *op. cit*.

these continentals were not mere satellites or conduits for Washington integration projects. The initial Beneluxer conversion and advocacy to multilateralism and integration appear to have been central, but the Swiss, Italian and Dutch participation after 1951 made the movement multilateral. Most of these histories support the thesis that France's decisions in 1948-49 were central to the "lift off" of integration, particularly for the smaller powers with their dual preoccupations about the German dilemma and their trading futures. The France-led integration decision that emphasized accommodative, but collective, economic policies, and institutions that incorporated Germany and moved without the British, was to be the most significant post-war integration decision. The support of France was again critical for the creation of the EC in 1955–57 in terms of willingness to compromise, as was the compelling power of the Federal Republic, particularly in its acceptance of the mediator power.[19]

The enlargement of the historical horizon to include the divergent European contributions to the genesis of integration has been important because it has questioned the original Western solidarity picture. This is true in terms of West European-American conflicting views abut the post-war order, exposed most fully by Bullock, Anderson and others, but in addition, about the fragmenting causes of inter-European difficulties. If the US sought firstly the diplomatic and political benefits of European economic stability, emphasizing the political gains of a Europe united, Europe's common goal appears now to have become meshing collective security and recovery as the basis for the *central* post-war need—region-based economic reorganization to compete globally. The existence of European integration initiatives sponsored by the continental elites, so well-defined by Lipgens, Loth, and the Poidevin contributors is no longer debatable. As a consequence of these historians, we know that there were fundamental clashes between the Anglo-American and emergent continental integration perspectives, both in form and rationale. We also see, as Lawrence Kaplan has put it, that Little Europeans were resolving European problems when *they* began to employ integrationist ideas. To them, American presence, power, commitment and support was there to support European innovation. The US might be the custodian of both peace and the world economy for the Europeans, but America could not be accepted as their governors and directors for the long term.

Who inspired, let alone what was the motor for the integration movement turns out to be the Americans at times, the Soviet threat at other times, but more than here or there, the historic Franco-German dilemma resolved within the new continental concept of banding together for future economic strength and diplomatic clout. In sum, the recent historiographical discoveries

---

[19]See H.V. KUSTERS in SERRA, *op. cit.*, which relates French participation in issues such as security, major powerful personalities, Euratom and the driving force of European political will.

suggest strongly that early post-war European activities were critically centered on the fundamental restructuring of economic attitudes and practices for the global trade competition. Acting in a bipolar world and responding to its limitations, the Western Europeans nevertheless conceived of an economic renaissance demanded by the post-war economic realities. Whether pointed toward closer economic cooperation or, more likely, economic sector or general integration, these visions represented impressive and unprecedented moves of collaboration. While deferring the immediate and too-ambitious goal of political unification, the Europeans debated the intricacies of economic integration and commenced the requisite institution-building.